Ramona Faith Oswald
Editor

Lesbian Rites: Symbolic Acts and the Power of Community

Lesbian Rites: Symbolic Acts and the Power of Community has been co-published simultaneously as *Journal of Lesbian Studies*, Volume 7, Number 2 2003.

Pre-publication
REVIEWS,
COMMENTARIES,
EVALUATIONS . . .

"INFORMATIVE, ENLIGHTENING, AND WELL WRITTEN . . . illuminates the range of lesbian ritual behavior in a creative and thorough manner. Ramona Faith Oswald and the contributors to this book have done scholars and students of ritual studies an important service by demonstrating the power, pervasiveness, and performative nature of lesbian ritual practices.

Cele Otnes, PhD
Associate Professor
Department of Business Administration
University of Illinois

Lesbian Rites:
Symbolic Acts and the Power of Community

Lesbian Rites: Symbolic Acts and the Power of Community has been co-published simultaneously as *Journal of Lesbian Studies*, Volume 7, Number 2 2003.

The *Journal of Lesbian Studies* Monographic "Separates"

Below is a list of "separates," which in serials librarianship means a special issue simultaneously published as a special journal issue or double-issue *and* as a "separate" hardbound monograph. (This is a format which we also call a "DocuSerial.")

"Separates" are published because specialized libraries or professionals may wish to purchase a specific thematic issue by itself in a format which can be separately cataloged and shelved, as opposed to purchasing the journal on an on-going basis. Faculty members may also more easily consider a "separate" for classroom adoption.

"Separates" are carefully classified separately with the major book jobbers so that the journal tie-in can be noted on new book order slips to avoid duplicate purchasing.

You may wish to visit Haworth's website at . . .

http://www.HaworthPress.com

. . . to search our online catalog for complete tables of contents of these separates and related publications.

You may also call 1-800-HAWORTH (outside US/Canada: 607-722-5857), or Fax 1-800-895-0582 (outside US/Canada: 607-771-0012), or e-mail at:

docdelivery@haworthpress.com

Lesbian Rites: Symbolic Acts and the Power of Community, edited by Ramona Faith Oswald, PhD (Vol. 7, No. 2 2003). *"INFORMATIVE, ENLIGHTENING, AND WELL WRITTEN . . . illuminates the range of lesbian ritual behavior in a creative and thorough manner. Ramona Faith Oswald and the contributors to this book have done scholars and students of ritual studies an important service by demonstrating the power, pervasiveness, and performative nature of lesbian ritual practices."* (Cele Otnes, PhD, Associate Professor, Department of Business Administration, University of Illinois)

Mental Health Issues for Sexual Minority Women: Re-Defining Women's Mental Health, edited by Tonda L. Hughes, RN, PhD, FAAN, Carrol Smith, RN, MS and Alice Dan, PhD (Vol. 7, No. 1 2003). *A rare look at mental health issues for lesbians and other sexual minority women.*

Addressing Homophobia and Heterosexism on College Campuses, edited by Elizabeth P. Cramer, PhD (Vol. 6, No. 3/4, 2002). *A practical guide to creating LGBT-supportive environments on college campuses.*

Femme/Butch: New Considerations of the Way We Want to Go, edited by Michelle Gibson and Deborah T. Meem (Vol. 6, No. 2, 2002). *"Disrupts the fictions of heterosexual norms. . . . A much-needed examiniation of the ways that butch/femme identitites subvert both heteronormativity and 'expected' lesbian behavior."* (Patti Capel Swartz, PhD, Assistant Professor of English, Kent State University)

Lesbian Love and Relationships, edited by Suzanna M. Rose, PhD (Vol. 6, No. 1, 2002). *"Suzanna Rose's collection of 13 essays is well suited to prompting serious contemplation and discussion about lesbian lives and how they are–or are not–different from others. . . . Interesting and useful for debunking some myths, confirming others, and reaching out into new territories that were previously unexplored."* (Lisa Keen, BA, MFA, Senior Political Correspondent, Washington Blade)

Everyday Mutinies: Funding Lesbian Activism, edited by Nanette K. Gartrell, MD, and Esther D. Rothblum, PhD (Vol. 5, No. 3, 2001). *"Any lesbian who fears she'll never find the money, time, or support for her work can take heart from the resourcefulness and dogged determination of the contributors to this book. Not only do these inspiring stories provide practical tips on making dreams come true, they offer an informal history of lesbian political activism since World War II."* (Jane Futcher, MA, Reporter, Marin Independent Journal, and author of Crush, Dream Lover, and Promise Not to Tell)

Lesbian Studies in Aotearoa/New Zealand, edited by Alison J. Laurie (Vol. 5, No. 1/2, 2001). *These fascinating studies analyze topics ranging from the gender transgressions of women pass-*

ing as men in order to work and marry as they wished to the effects of coming out on modern women's health.

Lesbian Self-Writing: The Embodiment of Experience, edited by Lynda Hall (Vol. 4, No. 4, 2000). *"Probes the intersection of love for words and love for women. . . . Luminous, erotic, evocative." (Beverly Burch, PhD, psychotherapist and author,* Other Women: Lesbian/Bisexual Experience and Psychoanalytic Views of Women *and* On Intimate Terms: The Psychology of Difference in Lesbian Relationships)

'Romancing the Margins'? Lesbian Writing in the 1990s, edited by Gabriele Griffin, PhD (Vol. 4, No. 2, 2000). *Explores lesbian issues through the mediums of books, movies, and poetry and offers readers critical essays that examine current lesbian writing and discuss how recent movements have tried to remove racist and anti-gay themes from literature and movies.*

From Nowhere to Everywhere: Lesbian Geographies, edited by Gill Valentine, PhD (Vol. 4, No. 1, 2000). *"A significant and worthy contribution to the ever growing literature on sexuality and space. . . . A politically significant volume representing the first major collection on lesbian geographies. . . . I will make extensive use of this book in my courses on social and cultural geography and sexuality and space." (Jon Binnie, PhD, Lecturer in Human Geography, Liverpool, John Moores University, United Kingdom)*

Lesbians, Levis and Lipstick: The Meaning of Beauty in Our Lives, edited by Jeanine C. Cogan, PhD, and Joanie M. Erickson (Vol. 3, No. 4, 1999). *Explores lesbian beauty norms and the effects these norms have on lesbian women.*

Lesbian Sex Scandals: Sexual Practices, Identities, and Politics, edited by Dawn Atkins, MA (Vol. 3, No. 3, 1999). *"Grounded in material practices, this collection explores confrontation and coincidence among identity politics, 'scandalous' sexual practices, and queer theory and feminism. . . . It expands notions of lesbian identification and lesbian community." (Maria Pramaggiore, PhD, Assistant Professor, Film Studies, North Carolina State University, Raleigh)*

The Lesbian Polyamory Reader: Open Relationships, Non-Monogamy, and Casual Sex, edited by Marcia Munson and Judith P. Stelboum, PhD (Vol. 3, No. 1/2, 1999). *"Offers reasonable, logical, and persuasive explanations for a style of life I had not seriously considered before. . . . A terrific read." (Beverly Todd, Acquisitions Librarian, Estes Park Public Library, Estes Park, Colorado)*

Living "Difference": Lesbian Perspectives on Work and Family Life, edited by Gillian A. Dunne, PhD (Vol. 2, No. 4, 1998). *"A fascinating, groundbreaking collection. . . . Students and professionals in psychiatry, psychology, sociology, and anthropology will find this work extremely useful and thought provoking." (Nanette K. Gartrell, MD, Associate Clinical Professor of Psychiatry, University of California at San Francisco Medical School)*

Acts of Passion: Sexuality, Gender, and Performance, edited by Nina Rapi, MA, and Maya Chowdhry, MA (Vol. 2, No. 2/3, 1998). *"This significant and impressive publication draws together a diversity of positions, practices, and polemics in relation to postmodern lesbian performance and puts them firmly on the contemporary cultural map." (Lois Keidan, Director of Live Arts, Institute of Contemporary Arts, London, United Kingdom)*

Gateways to Improving Lesbian Health and Health Care: Opening Doors, edited by Christy M. Ponticelli, PhD (Vol. 2, No. 1, 1997). *"An unprecedented collection that goes to the source for powerful and poignant information on the state of lesbian health care." (Jocelyn C. White, MD, Assistant Professor of Medicine, Oregon Health Sciences University; Faculty, Portland Program in General Internal Medicine, Legacy Portland Hospitals, Portland, Oregon)*

Classics in Lesbian Studies, edited by Esther Rothblum, PhD (Vol. 1, No. 1, 1996). *"Brings together a collection of powerful chapters that cross disciplines and offer a broad vision of lesbian lives across race, age, and community." (Michele J. Eliason, PhD, Associate Professor, College of Nursing, The University of Iowa)*

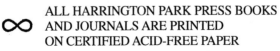

Lesbian Rites:
Symbolic Acts and the Power of Community

Ramona Faith Oswald, PhD
Editor

Lesbian Rites: Symbolic Acts and the Power of Community has been co-published simultaneously as *Journal of Lesbian Studies*, Volume 7, Number 2 2003.

Harrington Park Press
An Imprint of
The Haworth Press, Inc.
New York • London • Oxford

Published by

Harrington Park Press®, 10 Alice Street, Binghamton, NY 13904-1580 USA

Harrington Park Press® is an imprint of The Haworth Press, Inc., 10 Alice Street, Binghamton, NY 13904-1580 USA.

Lesbian Rites: Symbolic Acts and the Power of Community has been co-published simultaneously as *Journal of Lesbian Studies*, Volume 7, Number 2 2003.

The development, preparation, and publication of this work has been undertaken with great care. However, the publisher, employees, editors, and agents of The Haworth Press and all imprints of The Haworth Press, Inc., including The Haworth Medical Press® and The Pharmaceutical Products Press®, are not responsible for any errors contained herein or for consequences that may ensue from use of materials or information contained in this work. Opinions expressed by the author(s) are not necessarily those of The Haworth Press, Inc. With regard to case studies, identities and circumstances of individuals discussed herein have been changed to protect confidentiality. Any resemblance to actual persons, living or dead, is entirely coincidental.

Cover design by Marylouise E. Doyle

Library of Congress Cataloging-in-Publication Data

Lesbian rites : symbolic acts and the power of community / Ramona Faith Oswald, editor.
    p. cm.
    Co-published simultaneously as Journal of lesbian studies, v. 7, no. 2, 2003.
    Includes bibliographical references and index.
    ISBN 1-56023-314-1 (hard : alk. paper) – ISBN 1-56023-315-X (pbk. : alk. paper)
    1. Lesbianism. 2. Rites and ceremonies. I.Oswald, Ramona Faith. II. Journal of lesbian studies.
HQ75.5 .L4453 2002
306.76'63–dc21

    2002154182

Indexing, Abstracting & Website/Internet Coverage

This section provides you with a list of major indexing & abstracting services. That is to say, each service began covering this periodical during the year noted in the right column. Most Websites which are listed below have indicated that they will either post, disseminate, compile, archive, cite or alter their own Website users with research-based content from this work. (This list is as current as the copyright date of this publication.)

Abstracting, Website/Indexing Coverage......... Year When Coverage Began

- *Abstracts in Social Gerontology: Current Literature on Aging* 1997

- *CNPIEC Reference Guide: Chinese National Directory of Foreign Periodicals* 1997

- *Contemporary Women's Issues* 1998

- *e-psyche, LLC <www.e-psyche.net>* 2001

- *Family & Society Studies Worldwide <www.nisc.com>* 2001

- *Feminist Periodicals: A Current Listing of Contents* 1997

- *FINDEX <www.publist.com>* 1999

- *Gay & Lesbian Abstracts <www.nisc.com>* 1997

- *GenderWatch <www.slinfo.com>* 1999

- *HOMODOK/"Relevant" Bibliographic database, Documentation Centre for Gay & Lesbian Studies, University of Amsterdam (selective printed abstracts in "Homologie" and bibliographic computer databases covering cultural, historical, social, and political aspects of gay & lesbian topics)* 1997

(continued)

Special Bibliographic Notes related to special journal issues (separates) and indexing/abstracting:

- indexing/abstracting services in this list will also cover material in any "separate" that is co-published simultaneously with Haworth's special thematic journal issue or DocuSerial. Indexing/abstracting usually covers material at the article/chapter level.
- monographic co-editions are intended for either non-subscribers or libraries which intend to purchase a second copy for their circulating collections.
- monographic co-editions are reported to all jobbers/wholesalers/approval plans. The source journal is listed as the "series" to assist the prevention of duplicate purchasing in the same manner utilized for books-in-series.
- to facilitate user/access services all indexing/abstracting services are encouraged to utilize the co-indexing entry note indicated at the bottom of the first page of each article/chapter/contribution.
- this is intended to assist a library user of any reference tool (whether print, electronic, online, or CD-ROM) to locate the monographic version if the library has purchased this version but not a subscription to the source journal.
- individual articles/chapters in any Haworth publication are also available through the Haworth Document Delivery Service (HDDS).

Lesbian Rites:
Symbolic Acts and the Power
of Community

CONTENTS

ABOUT THE EDITOR

Ramona Faith Oswald, PhD, is Assistant Professor of Family Studies in the Department of Human Community Development at the University of Illinois. Her research examines queer family relationships especially through the lens of ritual, with attention to how community context shapes family dynamics. She has published in family, sociology, and psychology journals. Her work often has an applied component, for example you can find advice for heterosexual people planning weddings at *www.staff.uiuc.edu/~roswald*. Dr. Oswald is active within the National Council of Family Relations (NCFR), especially the Feminism and Family Studies Section and the Gay, Lesbian, Bisexual, Transgender, Straight Alliance Focus Group, which she co-founded. She has received two awards from NCFR: The Jesse Bernard Award for feminist research, and the Anslem Strauss Award for qualitative methodology. She and her partner are the proud co-moms of a beautiful baby boy.

Preface

Though in the last century much has been written about the role of ritual in reproducing social order, an emerging literature considers the ways in which ritual can promote social change (Baumann, 1992). It is within this emergent area that the study of lesbians and ritual belongs. By marking the importance of lesbian life transitions, reworking ethnic and religious symbolism to be inclusive, and defining family membership on lesbian terms, lesbian rituals sanctify lesbian existence. Ritual objects imbued with meaning can lend physical form to the idea of lesbian importance, and ritual interactions can establish ways of relating that center lesbian experience.

In this volume you will find five different explorations of ritual that bring forth themes of lesbian-centered social change. The first, "Death's Midwife" by Sharon Jaffe, is a narrative about the power of ritual to reconcile straight and gay, Christian and Pagan, in the face of dying. Ruth Rhiannon Barrett's exploration of Dianic traditions provides a brief history of the importance of Goddess-worship to radical lesbian feminists, and uses those traditions to create life-course rituals. While Barrett and Jaffe define "lesbians" and "lesbian community" very concretely, Marla Brettschneider disrupts notions of a static "lesbian self" and instead reworks Judaism and anarchist politics to propose rituals of continuous "becoming." Krista B. McQueeney then analyzes the paradoxes of a lesbian commitment ceremony held within a gay-affirmative African American congregation in the southern USA. Finally, Elizabeth A. Suter and I use exploratory survey data to examine how lesbians may use name changing as a strategy to claim family status.

Though it is tempting to think about ritual as a solely positive experience, there is nothing inherently good or bad about ritual. It is a powerful vehicle for reproducing or resisting social values and organization that can work for *or against* a particular group's interests (Baumann, 1992). The above-mentioned authors discuss the limits of ritual as part of their exploration. In addition, I have

[Haworth co-indexing entry note]: "Preface." Oswald, Ramona Faith. Co-published simultaneously in *Journal of Lesbian Studies* (Harrington Park Press, an imprint of The Haworth Press, Inc.) Vol. 7, No. 2, 2002, pp. xvii-xviii; and: *Lesbian Rites: Symbolic Acts and the Power of Community* (ed: Ramona Faith Oswald) Harrington Park Press, an imprint of The Haworth Press, Inc., 2002, pp. xi-xii. Single or multiple copies of this article are available for a fee from The Haworth Document Delivery Service [1-800-HAWORTH, 9:00 a.m. - 5:00 p.m. (EST). E-mail address: docdelivery@haworthpress.com].

included two papers that examine how lesbians have been compromised, if not harmed, by the ritualization of heterosexism and homophobia. First, in her analysis of the community response to the feminist retreat known as Camp Sister Spirit, Kate Greene uses Mary Daly's seven patterns of sado-ritual syndrome to show how those opposed to the camp were organized to uphold heterosexual patriarchy through an obsession with purity that defined the camp as a refuge for immorality, a rapid contagion of hateful expression that became both normalized and denied, and a public response that framed issues in stereotyped and unconstructive terms. Second, I include my own investigation of gay, lesbian, bisexual, and transgender (GLBT) people's experiences at heterosexual family weddings. Participants were pressured repeatedly to either diminish themselves or leave the ritual so that the heteronormative meaning of weddings and family membership would be upheld. The contrast between the first 5 papers and these 2 further illustrates the importance of lesbian-centered ritual practices.

This volume is, to the best of my knowledge, the first multidisciplinary compilation of scholarship addressing lesbians and ritual. The readings offer a diversity of perspectives on what it means to be lesbian, what it means to enact a ritual, what ritual is and is not able to accomplish, and how we should go about understanding lesbian ritual experiences. As editor, I worked to maintain the differences between authors. It is up to you, the reader, to debate and compare the perspectives presented by each. Together, they open the door to what I hope will be a vibrant and growing area of exploration.

Finally, I would like to offer my thanks to the people who were instrumental in creating this collection. First and foremost, I would like to thank Esther Rothblum for her encouragement and patience and Joan Laird for passing on the ritual torch to the next generation of scholars. Also, I am indebted to Grace Giorgio for her word-crafting talents and Alexis Daniel for her fire. Further, for their interest and rigor, I would like to thank Sharon Denham, Aine Humble, Melynda Huskey, Randi Levin, Robin Mathy, Patricia Nelson, Cele Otnes, Shannon Planck, Elizabeth Pleck, Michelle Renaud, Paul Rosenblatt, Leigh Saint-Louis, Jesook Song, and Denise Wilson. I would also like to recognize Haworth Press and Sage Publications for generously granting permission to reprint. And as always, I am grateful for Allie and she knows why.

Ramona Faith Oswald, Guest Editor

REFERENCE

Baumann, G. (1992). Ritual implicates others: Rereading Durkheim in a plural society. In D. DeCoppett (Ed.), *Understanding rituals* (pp. 97-116). New York: Routledge.

Introduction

Joan Laird

SUMMARY. In this introduction to the Oswald volume, it is argued that there is no politically correct way to design lesbian ritual. Lesbians create their own and participate in rituals that may be punctuated with traditional family of origin, religious, and cultural symbols as well as symbols and practices drawn from lesbian cultures. Lesbians, like everyone else, need to review their ritual lives, to construct rituals that are empowering rather than inhibiting or bereft of meaning, and to delete those that do not express their meanings. The authors herein richly describe and deconstruct a range of rituals participated in by lesbians, speculating on the ways they may be transforming and the ways they may be disaffirming. *[Article copies available for a fee from The Haworth Document Delivery Service: 1-800-HAWORTH. E-mail address: <docdelivery@haworthpress.com> Website: <http://www.HaworthPress.com> © 2003 by The Haworth Press, Inc. All rights reserved.]*

KEYWORDS. Ritual, lesbian, family

Several years ago, my son, Duncan, raised in a lesbian-headed family with a visiting father, was married. My lesbian partner and I, one on each side, accompanied him down the aisle. As we reached the front of the college chapel, we stopped and he gave each of us a long hug and a thank you. On one side of the chapel sat my daughter-in-law's family, mostly Jewish, and her invited

---

Joan Laird is Professor Emerita at the Smith College School for Social Work.

[Haworth co-indexing entry note]: "Introduction." Laird, Joan. Co-published simultaneously in *Journal of Lesbian Studies* (Harrington Park Press, an imprint of The Haworth Press, Inc.) Vol. 7, No. 2, 2003, pp. 1-6; and: *Lesbian Rites: Symbolic Acts and the Power of Community* (ed: Ramona Faith Oswald) Harrington Park Press, an imprint of The Haworth Press, Inc., 2003, pp. 1-6. Single or multiple copies of this article are available for a fee from The Haworth Document Delivery Service [1-800-HAWORTH, 9:00 a.m. - 5:00 p.m. (EST). E-mail address: docdelivery@haworthpress.com].

friends, mostly heterosexual. On the other side sat my partner's and my families, most of Protestant origin but religiously non-affiliated, and a mixture of our son's and our friends, many of whom were Jewish, and many of whom were gay. At the front of the chapel the chuppah was held aloft by four men: one Jew, one Arab, one Jehovah's Witness, and one not church affiliated. Two of the young men, my son's childhood friends from the midwest, had never seen or heard of a chuppah before. The young couple had designed the ceremony and written their own vows. The Unitarian minister, an 8-months pregnant woman, began by saying:

> Marriage is a privilege not available to every person in this society and we hope for a time when all people who love each other, gay and lesbian as well as heterosexual, may celebrate openly with their unions officially sanctioned by the government and blessed by all of the people.

The ritual they had created together was ecumenical, sprinkled with symbols and practices from various cultures that had meaning to them, as well as their own innovations. Their words and those of the minister were free of sexist or heterosexist language. Several family members and friends spoke and Kaddish was said. I commented on the strengths each brought to the union from his and her cultural traditions.

The wedding, which ended with the smashing of the glass, was followed by the reception. I danced with my partner, my son, the bride's father, with friends. So did my partner. Many women, both heterosexual and lesbian, danced with their partners or female friends (though males did not dance with other males), the dance floor a lively collection of old and young, heterosexual and gay. The joyous party continued well into the night. My daughter-in-law's family, raconteurs all, told many family marvelous stories, while one young man from the midwest, the Jehovah's Witness who had helped keep the chuppah aloft, came to the stage to say:

> I hadn't really planned to come up here. . . . (Duncan and I) both came from kind of unusual family backgrounds, but I want to tell you, no one I know has better parents than Duncan, and I would just like to say something to Ann and Joan about how much I appreciate what you did for him.

I briefly recount this event after carefully reading the articles in this volume on lesbian ritual, because they were so personally evocative, both affirming and challenging my own ideas about the power and meanings of ritual in general and lesbian ritual in particular. They pushed me to revisit some of my own ritual participation, to reminisce. In the process, I began to see some aspects a little differently, the texts provoking me toward reshaping meanings, editing and enriching my own life narrative.

I hadn't anticipated that my son's wedding would also become a public commitment ceremony, another step in the lifelong coming out process, for my partner and me. We were very moved. Although all of our heterosexual friends (and probably my son's friends over time) had come to understand that we were a lesbian couple, for a variety of reasons we had been verbally closeted for many, many years. Not only did the words and performance serve as a spoken and witnessed acknowledgement of our own thirty years together, but it also said to the community, "We are a lesbian family. Look, lesbians form stable families; they can raise splendid (and even heterosexual?!) children. Just look at the wonderful man we have produced, with his beautiful, talented bride!" That our family now included Jewish members brought delight and further connection with our Jewish friends. At least part of the tremendous expressions of joy that day seemed to be associated with new levels of commonality and sharing.

The wedding brought together people from many places and many moments from our lives, reinforcing and reforming a powerful experience of communitas. Krista McQueeney, in this issue, makes the point that not everyone is transformed through ritual and that the same ritual may hold very different meanings for each participant. For example, one of my brothers and his wife left the reception early, caught a flight early the next day, and later told my mother they hadn't liked the wedding. Although unfortunately we've never spoken about this, my hunch is that the personalized nature of the ceremony and the flagrant display of gay talk and dancing–perhaps even the presence of so many Jewish people and symbols–were outside of their experience. Not only were they personally offended, the entire ritual defied their very right wing personal and political views, which in turn thrive on sexist, heterosexist, and racist ideologies. All but one of their children has had "boilerplate" weddings, or what some call "rent-a-wedding." By contrast, most of our lesbian friends were ecstatic, several saying they couldn't believe it, surely they thought they had died and gone to heaven. For the most part from a formerly closeted generation and some still silent about their sexuality, several of our closest lesbian friends have not had commitment ceremonies themselves and have often felt alienated and invisible at such events. This ritual also served as an affirmation for them and their life choices. For us and for an older generation of lesbians, it was indeed transformative, if not revolutionary. Some lesbians, who may view long term and exclusive commitment as a conservative capitulation to patriarchal and heterosexual values, might also have been uncomfortable on this occasion.

Two other aspects of this ritual may help to frame my comments about lesbian ritual in relation to some of the themes raised in these uniformly splendid articles. First, my daughter-in-law sent in their engagement notice to the *New York Times*. The society page editor informed her that they could not include my partner's name as one of our son's parents; it wasn't done. She was very distressed and angry, and had decided not to make the announcement in the *Times*. At the time, gay men and lesbians in the obituary section could be "survived" by a gay partner, but not raised by one. OK dead, not alive. Another potentially toxic issue came up around their wedding invitation. Both my son's father and his fiancée's mother had recently died. Her father had remarried, so that she had a relatively new stepmother. Who should be included on the invitation? In the first situation, we urged that my daughter-in-law go ahead with the announcement, deciding that we would complain to the *Times*. In the second situation, when asked, in spite of the fact that generally I probably would have said it was up to them, in this instance I was able to say that I felt very strongly that my partner should be acknowledged. (After all, she had supported and raised my son for most of his life, and we together were paying for half of the wedding! No sexists we!) She was there, on the invitation, for all to see.

I suspect the articles herein will evoke many different feelings and reflections on the part of each of you, too, as well as stimulate new questions. Some of the haunting questions for me are: What makes a lesbian ritual "lesbian"? Is it because it is lesbians who perform it? Or because it contains various actions or symbols that are uniquely lesbian? For that matter, what makes a wedding or a funeral or a bat mitzvah heterosexual or "traditional?" What makes it transformative or even revolutionary, or, on the other hand, hollow and stultifying? What happens to the witnesses of ritual? Why is the same wedding empowering and transforming for some, and distasteful for others? For whom is a sense of communitas strengthened? Which witnesses feel more alienated, and why? Is ritual always a definitional and political act?

Behind these questions lies another, even more fundamental, set of questions, having to do with the very meanings of lesbianism. What is a lesbian? Or, more accurately, what does (be)coming a lesbian through ritual mean? These and many other provocative questions are approached throughout these pages. Some authors explore lesbian experiences in rituals created specifically for women in general and lesbians in particular–rituals that create separate space and patriarchy-defying practices such as those drawing on Dianic traditions or part of a unique community such as Camp Sister Spirit. Others analyze the blending of tradition and innovation in lesbian commitment and healing/dying rituals. Some authors give special attention to the political aspects of ritual, and raise questions about what is transformative or uniquely lesbian and what may be imitative of heterosexual ritual. Ramona Oswald, editor of this volume, explores how lesbians find or do not find relevant meanings for their own lives in the heterosexual family wedding. In the process, she makes several important points that I believe are crucial to any understanding of lesbians and ritual. The first point (which one would not think would need to be made) is that all GLBT people are not necessarily alike. I would add that all heterosexual people are not alike, that both lesbianism and heterosexuality, as Brettschneider argues, are "identities produced through their very enactments." Second, many aspects of ritual, such as the expression of commitment or dancing or the promise of monogamy, are not necessarily heterosexual or patriarchal. And third, we should not assume that families are either straight or gay. Lesbian-headed families often have straight members; straight-headed families most often have one or more lesbian or gay relatives perched on the family tree. Whether central actors in the drama, or members of the audience, each participant, as both Kenneth Burke and Barbara Myerhoff have said, "dances an attitude." Rituals can be experienced as meaningless, or worse, oppressive. Many lesbians have been unable to find their own meanings expressed in what for them are empty or sexist, heterosexist, spiritually, or culturally alienating exercises. Others, whether lesbian, gay, bisexual, or transgendered, may find rituals designed by people of their same identity express experiences and values profoundly different from their own, for there is no such thing as a single "lesbian" culture. Rituals can be transformative and even revolutionary, expressing the past and also challenging the normative, but only if they validate one's own meanings and hopes, if they do not impose unfamiliar or alienating values and practices.

I believe we err when we cede "tradition" to the world of heterosexuality, or when we either exaggerate or minimize the differences between human beings of different ethnicities or social classes or sexualities. As lesbians, although we need to celebrate what may be particularly ours, we do not spring from some cultural vacuum, bereft of meaningful traditions, plots, stories, rituals, and other sources to mine for the building of our own life narratives. There is nothing innately heterosexual about loving a child, solving problems, mourning a loss, or becoming a parent. Intimacy, commitment, spirituality, religious belief, dancing, taking vows, dealing with losses and separations, celebrating achievements, and so on are not owned by heterosexuals. To incorporate aspects of our cultural heritages, perhaps learned in our heterosexual-headed families, in the ways we love, or parent, or celebrate, or mourn is not to imitate heterosexuality. Just as the butch woman does not simply imitate masculinity, just as some lesbian couples' daily rituals may resemble those they learned in their mainly heterosexual households or those of their heterosexual neighbors, such performances do not necessarily represent the evils of patriarchy or heteronormativity. There is no politically correct way to design lesbian ritual. Rituals punctuated with traditional cultural or religious symbols may be just as affirming, transformative, and meaningful in relation to (be)coming lesbian as are those associated with particular lesbian cultures. There are many lesbian cultures and many ways to be lesbian, each of us trying to be true to our own lived experiences. Many heterosexual women are revisioning Christmas, Passover, the Mikvah bath, their weddings, their work and household rituals in ways that are empowering rather than demeaning or limiting. The point resides in the ability to choose, which, to paraphrase Foucault, may demand the insurrection of subjugated knowledge. We need to repeatedly interrogate and deconstruct our cultural narratives and practices, deleting those ritual practices that may inhibit or disempower us, and replacing them with rituals that do fit with what we value from the past and hope for in the future.

That is what the talented scholars in this collection do. They interrogate how lesbians shape their own rituals in ways that express and create their constantly emerging identities and the ways they participate in what are typically thought of as heterosexual or larger cultural religious and secular rituals, often reclaiming them in new ways. It is, as I wrote some time ago, a matter of *bricolage*, a term used by Levi-Strauss to mean the combining and incorporating in our rituals and life narratives fragments of meaning from many sources.

Death's Midwife

Sharon Jaffe

SUMMARY. Ritual provided a way for Nance, her lesbian family, and her birth family to care for each other during Nance's diagnosis and death of cancer. "Death's Midwife" tells of the Tuesday night healing rituals and some of the rituals during Nance's dying days. The survivors used ritual in grief and in the memorial service; however, once Nance died the ritual circle fragmented. This short memoir examines how lesbian-created ritual centered, for a while, a lesbian family and community. *[Article copies available for a fee from The Haworth Document Delivery Service: 1-800-HAWORTH. E-mail address: <docdelivery@haworthpress.com> Website: <http://www.HaworthPress.com> © 2003 by The Haworth Press, Inc. All rights reserved.]*

KEYWORDS. Ritual, lesbian, death/grief, Jewish, pagan

The rose quartz pyramid Nance gave me the Thursday night before she died has been sheathed in silk since then. Thirteen years. Just now, telling this story, it calls to come out. I place it on my seventh chakra, balance it on top of my head. Subtle vibrations move through me. The base orients to the four directions. The top points to the air, the Universe. An image of food, a plate of steamed vegetables. Judging that a bit disrespectful, I lift off the pyramid. Place it on a red rock. One red rock among a ring of rocks around a little used fire pit. The fire pit is under trees, which always irks me. I like watching flames and stars. Trees obstruct the view. Today the trees shelter me from a blazing

---

[Haworth co-indexing entry note]: "Death's Midwife." Jaffe, Sharon. Co-published simultaneously in *Journal of Lesbian Studies* (Harrington Park Press, an imprint of The Haworth Press, Inc.) Vol. 7, No. 2, 2003, pp. 7-14; and: *Lesbian Rites: Symbolic Acts and the Power of Community* (ed: Ramona Faith Oswald) Harrington Park Press, an imprint of The Haworth Press, Inc., 2003, pp. 7-14. Single or multiple copies of this article are available for a fee from The Haworth Document Delivery Service [1-800-HAWORTH, 9:00 a.m. - 5:00 p.m. (EST). E-mail address: docdelivery@haworthpress.com].

July sun. I am grateful. I am happy to be alone on my lover's land. Amazed that it is three miles due west from the farm that Nance, other friends, and I rented in Wisconsin a long time ago.

This hot, windy day is the fire of summer. In the fire pit on the gray ash are the animals, small and carved or molded. They exist as a circle. Pewter dragon, east. Obsidian coyote, south. Malachite fox, west. Obsidian bear, north. A jade turtle travels round the circle. Today, this turtle carved from wood and painted with a bright sun on its shell lumbers in the northeast. Beyond the turtle, near the rose quartz pyramid, stands a finger-sized goddess with opal nipples. All these stand in ash. They stand in ash in a circle. I turn two rings on my fingers, slip them off. Rings that Nance wore and bequeathed to me. I lay them in the circle's center. Silver rings with stone, lapis, opal. Out beyond the circle, on the faggot, the burnt wood left from the last fire, on that wood lies Nance's death rattle. Ugly, beautiful, hand knitted sock stuck on a cornhusk. Bells dangle. Thirteen years old. Thirteen years dead.

Nance was my heart mate, a soul sister. We had five years full of outrageous laughter. We put ourselves in front of war mongers, danced late at night with other Lesbians, talked about who was zooming who, comforted each other through love's trials, and sang late at night around fires, either up on Minnesota's north shore of Lake Superior or out at our rented farm in Wisconsin. That farm reminded her of her childhood. No running water. No furnace. Heat from a wood stove floated up to the bedrooms through a small slot in the rough floorboards. A large garden. Stars bright at night. Snuggling with her sister in their one bed, snuggling with me winter nights near the stove drum. I loved her full laugh and vibrant face full of expression. Though we were never lovers, I enjoyed her always active body. She constantly did chores or errands or cooked or weeded.

We met on a bus that ferried women from the Twin Cities to the Seneca Women's Encampment for a Future of Peace and Justice. I was the new girl in town and got on the bus late. I walked up the aisle, past rows of Lesbians wearing the famous jeans and tee shirt look. Most of them had short blonde hair, very blonde. Self-conscious of my summer dress, and my long wavy dark hair, I stumbled into the direct glare of a woman wearing a puffy pink cap, a bit older than anyone else seemed, with an empty seat nearby. Her look challenged me to sit beside her. After I settled in, she questioned me, "Which affinity group would you be joining, the women's spirituality middle class affinity group?" "Well," I answered, "I had considered the working class one." Her eyebrows arched up fast, but, I said quickly, "but I decided that since the women's spirituality group will do direct action, I'll try that one." I have a fondness for feisty Lesbians and her big grin kept me going. "After all, I'm a garden variety Jewish Lesbian Feminist Activist, in transit to organic." She gasped for air through her laughter. "Stop, stop," she demanded. "I'll pee in my pants." That's how we began, testing and being tested.

Valentine's Day 1988 she called me from her bookkeeping job at the co-op. "My doctor just called. That frigging pain in my shoulder is not a bum rib, not a heart thing, is not even a fancy kind of arthritis kicking in just before menopause. It is cancer." "O dear," I spoke into the silence, my heart clogged with fear. "Ok, want me to come get you? Walk around a lake? Drive out to the farm?" I'm a distraction queen. She, however, would have none of that. "No. Call everyone and tell them to meet me at my house tonight." She listed friends, lovers, ex-lovers, co-workers, coven folk.

Nance called her kin to her . . . and we responded. Most of us were Lesbians, some not. Most of us had years of Wiccan spirituality in covens or during anti-nuclear, anti-U.S. intervention actions. Some were familiars in a formal coven. Some were Lesbians who had been on the edge of entering the Sisters of St. Joseph's–known in the Twin Cities for the radical nuns protesting U.S. military madness.

When Nance convened us that first Tuesday night, she cast the circle. She created the context for the next nine months and affirmed ritual as a mother tongue. For women in the circle new to that language . . . they learned quick. The shared intimacy, the pull into a life and death loving in this very moment, the opening to raw emotion and the trust in the natural process, all while spitting at the environmental and governmental outrages, all of that swept women into the ritual current.

That first Tuesday evening a bevy of women clustered around the knowledge that cancer ate at Nance. We greeted each other in the living room, wandered to the kitchen. Women's hands prepared foods. Put food in bowls. Set plates and utensils on the dining room table. At some point women congregated in the back room upstairs. We stood tightly packed together staring out the window looking at the alley, the weed trees, the trash. A full moon rose over the garage. Really. We howled. Hung onto each other. Voiced our desperation. Spent, we slowly paraded downstairs to become a heap on the living room couch. Nance sat swarmed with women massaging her head, arms, back, legs. I sat at her feet, aloof from the cluster of women. I touched her soles. We closed in silence, passed hugs around, and agreed to return.

We created a rhythm. On Tuesday nights women came. We cast a circle, chanted, raised energy. Then Nance said what she needed: Could be to rage. Could be to grieve. Could be to rattle off one blessing after another. Could be to direct us to console her. Could be to pick a tarot card that would guide her through the fears. Then women in the circle had a turn for asking. Could be rage. Could be consolation. We figured out who would bring Nance dinner, or learn about oncologists, or alternative therapies, or schedule appointments and getting friends to go with. . . . One of my consistent tasks was to advocate with Nance in the welfare system since the co-op paid no health care and she had no money. We chanted some more and in closing the circle each woman spoke about hope for healing and about the different ways love embraces fear. The different ways that love opens our hearts to each other.

Through the spring and early summer, kin from outside the Twin Cities came to visit. Nance had the chutzpah to demand that her blood kin accept her on her own terms. They were well used to loving her. Her older brother, a successful veterinarian from Phoenix, took us out to dinner–a dinner sandwiched between a Minnesota National Guard Out of Honduras demo and posting bail for one of the Tuesday night regulars. He just took it all in stride, silently. No judgment. In May her father took me aside to tell me whatever made Nance comfortable was for the best. One Tuesday night Nance showed us a picture her son's fiancé sent her: cancer cells lined up at the unemployment center. Nance had told her of our Tuesday night rituals and she drew a ritual image for us. Nance appreciated this give and take among people in her life.

After a remission, after an argument while driving back from Michigan in over 100 degree heat, where I said, "you're dying" and she said, "bullshit," after she went to California for a week to try an intensive macrobiotic regime with her other heart mate who lived in Albuquerque, Nance ended up in the hospital. I decorated the room with scarves and goddess figures. The Tuesday night circle painted a pentagram on the window. Hung crystals. We crafted a variety of rituals in the hospital though Nance banished anger in her presence. She had no patience for it any longer. In the hospital, Nance presented each of us with gifts. Embroidered wall hangings, knitted orbs, macramé plant holders with special crystals, small woven scenes of gardens. Words to a song. She gave me a homemade rattle.

By then the we of Nance's family included her Lesbian family and her family of origin: her father, mother, and her twenty-year-old son raised by her parents. They came up from Missouri and rented a short-term apartment in Minneapolis. Our Tuesday night circle befriended her parents, played cards or went out for dinner. They were Christians. We were a mix of Wiccans and Jews. The dance of becoming an us was easy, inspired by Nance's love. We respected each other's spiritual ways. We communicated. Somehow it was normal. It didn't seem unusual. It was seamless as breathing.

The second day in the hospital the chaplain, the social worker, and the nurses hovered over Nance like vultures, albeit good-natured ones. Ready to help, but expecting grievous tension, or perhaps, sheer nastiness between the two families. But the two families shared the moment, our present tense, and our mutual comfort as preparation for the coming death. We Lesbians found a congregation for her parents after the hospital staff misinterpreted their working class language. Later, I understood how unique it was to cross cultural divides, how much just the act of these two families coming together was a source of healing for many Lesbians facing homophobia and cancer. O, we experienced homophobia and lesbophobia. From the oncologist. In the hospital. In the cremation society. But in the time of dying Nance insisted on a grace. Not a truce. The real grace of living each moment with a beloved.

She died of cancer at home. That last day, the second Friday in October 1988, a brilliant, gold day, I could touch the tumor on her throat. Another tumor bulged out from her belly. She couldn't breathe. Couldn't swallow. Her arms and legs moved that day in ways completely alien to human arms and legs. In death, she was turning into something unknown.

The night before she died, a Thursday night, I had been with her alone, in her bedroom at home. I read *Winnie the Pooh* in a soft voice. She asked me about the state of the world. I told her Chile might be holding people accountable for Allende's murder. She nodded, "Maybe I'll go there next, see for myself." I hummed a lullaby. She roused herself enough to ask me to pick up her rose quartz pyramid. After putting it on her heart, she offered it to me. We held it cupped in both our hands as she drifted off to sleep. I went home, napped, woke early, dressed for death. A pink skirt. A purple and green silk scarf, a birthday present from her. I drove over to the Mississippi. Stood in the rising sunlight. Took strength offered from the trees, the river. I went to her place, her bedroom. She was up, waiting for me. The panic in her eyes eased a little. I held her. Stroked her soft body. Nuzzled her shoulder. My nose tickled the tumor.

The door opened and to my amazement Lesbian after Lesbian entered the room. I found out later that she had called me while I was standing at the river in sunrise. My roommate, one of her ex-lovers, took Nance's directive and called the Tuesday night circle. I had wanted her to myself, had wanted the tenderness of comforting her within the shelter of our intimacy. Gone. Nance shifted into a more collective endeavor. She pulled two rings off her fingers and handed them to me. She radiated love.

Thirteen of us sat around the bed. She sang. We sang. We washed her body, dressed her. We listened to her wish to face death directly, with our assistance. It was clear that she was actively dying. It was only a matter of a slow starvation, hours or days. We already knew some options, had gathered up little bits of information, and together concocted a plan.

Some things don't go according to plan. Women in the circle feared the legal implications of what Nance wanted, Nance who chose her time and place to die. The intrusion of fear, fear of the Powers That Be, fear eroded the plan, changed it. Then her family of origin arrived. This was the only time they came without an expressed invite from Nance. She was protecting them from the act of death. But, a powerful intuitive sense motivated them to arrive that afternoon. Throughout the day women chanted constantly, "We all come from the water and to her we shall return like a drop of rain flowing to the ocean. . . ." Her mother sat at the foot of her bed. Her father and son like archangels on either side. One of the loves of her life and I took turns holding her as we sat behind her, supporting and cradling her. She nestled up to our breasts, our hearts. Her love so tangible you just drank it in, let it fill each cell with wonder. With love, women in the circle said good night. Her parents, son, and brother left Nance and me alone. They dozed in the living room. Just after midnight Nance breathed her last sweet breath.

The metro paper ran an article near the obituaries. The headline was in super large font: "Lesbian Activist and Teacher" accompanied by a picture of Nance from the MN Women's Peace Camp. The memorial service was a very public event. Both families planned it. Her father and brother called the circle's care, touch, and support a holy act of love. We settled on a Wiccan style. Cast a circle. Raise energy. Invoke the ancestors. People from various parts of Nance's life shared stories. Over 200 people attended.

During the memorial someone stood up and railed at us: "What did we think we were doing? Why wasn't there a minister or some clergy? Who were we to lead a memorial service? What about respect for her parents?" On and on. Anger. Rage. At the unfamiliar ritual. At an untimely death. For me, it was quite a disconcerting moment to be inside the circle and to experience this challenge to our authority. Nance would certainly have approved both the challenge and our steadfastness. The memorial ritual gave Lesbians permission in the years following to be OUT there when Lesbians died. To name our own kin. To practice our own empowering grief and its varied forms. To trust Lesbian community.

Nance started the Tuesday night circles. Healing ritual circles. There was a rhythm. Ritual often generates rhythm, or perhaps, I notice rhythms when I invoke ritual. Ritual acts a prism, shattering the illusion that light is white, a prism refracts light into a range of color. Ritual language articulates a range of time cycles, life cycles or communal calendars. It also attends to continuums of traditional or normative culture intersecting with the challenges inherent in living out Lesbian Feminist visions and values. Ritual sustained us through the knowledge, treatment, dying, and honoring our dead. Ritual, however, did not sustain an ad-hoc kinship circle over the grieving months and years.

Nance's ritual circle met one last time, Hallowmass, Halloween. We spun into separate orbits without Nance. That same spark that had ignited during the memorial service . . . how dare any of us take power in our own hands . . . how dare we step out of the Norm, whatever that is . . . how dare anyone soothe a natural process . . . sparks ignited. Fear burned. The flames of the Burning

Times, women burnt at the stake, the fear of consequences for being wild women, that fear burned hot.

I needed centering, cleansing. Death on my hands, grief in all my body/ mind/heart. My coven, some of us at the core of the healing rituals, dispersed. We couldn't find ways to help each other through the grieving; we couldn't find ways to heal from being that close to death. We tried. Tensions emerged. I was accused of having controlled access to Nance, also of endangering people in the circle if I told the bones of her death. The courage that had sustained our circle ebbed away. Still a layer of Lesbian community, a bedrock of strength from Nance's death endures. Through the decade's distance, Lesbians from the circle acknowledge each other with compassion.

How did I face the tensions, the fragmented circle, the loss of a heart mate, and the changed rhythms of my life? Yom Kippur came very late that year, it can't have been in November but I clearly remember that after Nance's death I went to services, Yiskor, the memorial service. I was called to the bimah to hold the Torah. This is an honor. Traditionally, those close to death don't come near the Torah. Traditionally, women don't come near the Torah. The sense of being not quite taboo, not quite impure, so close to death. I hesitated. Me, a midwife for death. I held the Torah. I chanted the shemah, the Jewish prayer of unity. I heard the congregation's response. The prayer of unity. My tears wet the Torah. Grateful for the power to enter into a tradition, for the power to challenge it, sorrow for my silence that I couldn't begin to say what I felt, sorrow that the Wiccan tradition, at least in that moment, couldn't offer me such a call and response, Lesbians couldn't hold the circle, gratitude for the personal healing, and sorrow, for my grief, my tears.

I followed Nance's lead in her call for radical self-determination within a loving community. One way was to join a group of dedicated women to envision, birth, and guide the Minnesota Women's Cancer Resource Center for its first three years. I learned to encourage Lesbians, to applaud our own authority during rituals we create to mark life's transitions. I know the struggles for inclusion of GLBT people in organized religion is important, and indeed it was through Jewish liturgy that I found solace, but I love ritual best where Lesbians transform it with our own organic spiritual languages, whatever they may be.

I write this to honor Nance's legacy and I hope this forum furthers our collective knowledge and practices. That's why I cast a circle in the cold fire pit on a blazing hot day, put Nance's rings in the center, and craft these words.

Nance and the Tuesday night circles served as catalyst and inspiration for many Lesbians in our community. There had been another, almost ten years before, whose kin had also generated ritual as she endured and died from cancer. There would be others, many, too many.

Ritual can transmit cultural realities through generations. What kinds of generative culture mark Lesbians? The legacy of closets, deviance, outsider? The legacy of sexual knowledge, the powers to name our realities, desires? The activism to counter the prevailing Patriarchal White Supremacist culture? A range of kinship structures that evoke community and bridge communities? Lesbians hand down the stories of our shared lives for a next generation, not necessarily meaning a biologically derived next generation. I know we are now generating rituals that will be recognizable across generations. With hope I hold Nance's death rattle, my hands clammy against the dried out corn husk. The animals in the circle, the silver rings in the center, the stories told. I shake the rattle. Listen. Do you hear?

B'shalom. Meaning, be whole, holy, well, welcome. B'shalom and blessed be.

Lesbian Rituals and Dianic Tradition

Ruth Rhiannon Barrett

SUMMARY. In her article, "Lesbian Rituals and Dianic Tradition," Dianic priestess Ruth Rhiannon Barrett, provides a herstorical perspective of the feminist Dianic Wiccan Goddess tradition and its contributions to lesbian culture. The article describes the cosmology of this Goddess-centered and women-identified magical denomination, and the figure of the Goddess Diana as a symbol of women free from patriarchal influences. Barrett's position is that lesbians can heal from, and challenge, internalized and externalized homophobia by creating and sharing in rituals that celebrate significant passages in their lives. Barrett discusses the personal and political importance of ritual-making as a way to honoring and valuing lesbian lives, otherwise invisible in the dominant

---

Ruth Rhiannon Barrett is a Dianic high priestess, ritualist, educator, musician, and award-winning recording artist of original Goddess-oriented songs. With her life partner, Falcon River, Ruth co-founded the Temple of Diana, Inc. Contact her online at: <info@templeofdiana.org>.

Ruth studied with Shekhinah Mountainwater, Z Budapest, and others in the early 1970s, and has been teaching Feminist Witchcraft and ritual-making internationally since her ordination by Z Budapest in 1980. Ruth served as religious director of Circle of Aradia, a local chapter of Re-formed Congregation of the Goddess in Los Angeles from 1993-2000. Her recently completed book, *Women's Rites, Women's Mysteries: Creating Personal and Group Ritual,* is awaiting publication. She has also contributed a chapter on "The Power of Ritual" that was published in *Daughters of the Goddess* (2000, Alta Mira Press, edited by Wendy Griffin).

In 1997, Ruth received the L.A.C.E. award for outstanding contributions in the area of Spirituality from the Gay and Lesbian Center in Los Angeles.

[Haworth co-indexing entry note]: "Lesbian Rituals and Dianic Tradition." Barrett, Ruth Rhiannon. Co-published simultaneously in *Journal of Lesbian Studies* (Harrington Park Press, an imprint of The Haworth Press, Inc.) Vol. 7, No. 2, 2003, pp. 15-28; and: *Lesbian Rites: Symbolic Acts and the Power of Community* (ed: Ramona Faith Oswald) Harrington Park Press, an imprint of The Haworth Press, Inc., 2003, pp. 15-28. Single or multiple copies of this article are available for a fee from The Haworth Document Delivery Service [1-800-HAWORTH, 9:00 a.m. - 5:00 p.m. (EST). E-mail address: docdelivery@haworthpress.com].

culture. Drawing upon 30 years of experience, Barrett provides examples from a spectrum of rituals that have been created: coming out, preparing to enter the circle of mothers, and honoring women's conscious choice not to have children.*[Article copies available for a fee from The Haworth Document Delivery Service: 1-800-HAWORTH. E-mail address: <docdelivery@haworthpress.com> Website: <http://www.HaworthPress.com> © 2003 by The Haworth Press, Inc. All rights reserved.]*

KEYWORDS. Ritual, lesbian, Dianic tradition, feminist spirituality

On Winter Solstice 1971, in a small, smoky apartment in Hollywood, California, Hungarian born Zsuzsanna E. Budapest led the first Dianic ritual for the Los Angeles women's community. A hereditary witch and visionary feminist whose spiritual activism eventually brought Goddess religion to second-wave U.S. feminists, Z Budapest is viewed largely as the mother of feminist Dianic Wiccan tradition (Eller, 2000; Griffin, in press; Noonan, 1998). She was the first to blend feminism with the Eastern European folk magic traditions of her mother (Noonan, 1998) and Goddess spirituality, into what she coined "feminist spirituality." On that night, the small circle of women poured feminist values and goddess religion into the cauldron of change and Dianic tradition was ignited, giving a life-quickening jolt of energy to the growth of what has become known as feminist Witchcraft.

Concurrently, feminist scholars, activists, writers, artists and musicians began to speak, publish, and create art, music, and song, inspired by Goddess iconography, mythology, feminist politics, and/or intuitive knowing. The works of "out" lesbians, and straight feminists, Shekhinah Mountainwater, Merlin Stone, Judy Chicago, Ruth and Jean Mountaingrove, the activist women of WITCH, Mary Daly, and Kay Gardner inspired others and added to the growing tide of Goddess consciousness (Eller, 2000; Griffin, 2000). Books like *When God Was A Woman* (Stone, 1976), *The Great Cosmic Mother* (Sjoo & Moor, 1987), *The Holy Book of Women's Mysteries* (Budapest, 1979), *The Spiral Dance* (Starhawk, 1979), *The Chalice and the Blade* (Eisler, 1988), and *Beyond God the Father* (Daly, 1973) carried the women's spirituality movement and feminist spirituality movement into the bookstores of mainstream America.

The work of archeologist Dr. Marija Gimbutas provided an academic contribution to the body of intuitive knowledge women held in their hearts. She argued that the original understanding and experience of what the dominant culture calls God was first worshipped as a Goddess. Dr. Gimbutas authored many books on ancient Goddess worshipping civilizations that gave compelling evidence of the widespread existence of a Neolithic Goddess-centered culture in pre-patriarchal Europe (e.g., Gimbutas, 1974). Although her work is controversial and disputed in some academic circles, many practitioners of Goddess spirituality are thankful to Marija Gimbutas for the inspiration her work brought forward regardless of whether some believe she attributed more opinion than the evidence supported (Griffin, in press).

During my studies in Folklore at the University of California, Santa Cruz from 1974-76, I sought information about the Goddess from the university library. At the same time, I apprenticed with Shekhinah Mountainwater in her home, called the Moon Hut, in the redwoods. By 1976, in Los Angeles, I had met Z Budapest, and was soon initiated into the Susan B. Anthony Coven #1. On Halloween night 1980, I was ordained as a high priestess by Z Budapest who planned to relocate to Northern California. She charged me with continuing her spiritual work in Los Angeles. It was a time of enormous creativity fueled by women's awakening to feminism, Goddess consciousness, lesbian identity for many, and woman-identification for all (Noonan, 1998). Being an observing participant (Adler & Adler, 1987) for almost 30 years, I have witnessed this merging of feminist politics and Goddess spirituality in ritual and the arts. I have been privileged to participate in, and contribute to, the evolution of Dianic tradition through teaching feminist Witchcraft and ritual-making within my spiritual community in Los Angeles and internationally. As information about the Goddess and feminist Witchcraft became more available, the numbers of heterosexual and bisexual women who became interested in Dianic and other Goddess-centered feminist traditions increased. My own students and spiritual community reflected this change as the years passed.

In 1993, I decided to incorporate my growing spiritual community in Los Angeles, Circle of Aradia, as a chapter of Re-formed Congregation of the Goddess International (RCGI). Circle of Aradia is the largest Dianic community in the United States, serving thousands of women over the last twenty years. Presently, Circle of Aradia is comprised of woman-identified feminist women with diverse sexual identities. Re-formed Congregation of the Goddess International is a feminist spirituality organization with predominantly lesbian members, and headquarters in Madison, Wisconsin. In the Minneapolis chapter of RCGI, approximately 75% of its participants are heterosexual but welcoming to lesbians (Jade, personal conversation). In spite of greater numbers of heterosexual and bisexual women's interest and participation in Dianic tradition, women who identify themselves as Dianic to other Wiccans are usually assumed to be lesbian. I have been repeatedly told that in Great Britain, to say one is Dianic is to say you are a lesbian feminist witch, and historically, this is true for the majority (Griffin, in press). My new organization, Temple of Diana, Inc. serves all women-identified women who wish to learn and practice Dianic tradition or train to be Dianic clergy.

Dianic tradition is known for its women-only ritual, exclusive focus on the Goddess in cosmology and magical practice (as compared to Wiccan traditions that operate on a male/female duality and worship the Goddess and a male consort), and its inclusion of contemporary feminist consciousness, values, and visions interwoven into the ritual content. The spiritual focus and ritual practices of Dianic tradition are woman-centered in that they are practiced with, for, and about women and women's experience of life. Dianic tradition's Goddess-centered cosmology, ethics, eclectic practices and rituals, are shaped and inspired by fragments of ancient Goddess worship, folklore, invention, and adaptation of other Wiccan practices [particularly from the writings of Gerald Gardner and Robert Graves (Hutton, 1999, Griffin, in press)].

The heart of Dianic spiritual practice focuses on Women's Mysteries. These rites of passage include the essential physical, emotional, and psychic transitions that only women born with female bodies can experience. These are the five uterine blood mysteries: being born, menarche, giving birth/lactation, menopause, and death, which acknowledge women's ability to create life, sustain life, and return our bodies to the Goddess in death. Dianic rituals also celebrate the earth's seasonal cycles of birth, death and regeneration, as it is reflected in women's own life cycles, and not on an exclusively heterosexual fertility cycle. Dianic tradition specifically includes the creation of rituals whose intention is to help women heal from, and counter the effects of misogynist, patriarchal social institutions and religions (Barrett, in press; Noonan, 1998).

In the early years of the Dianic movement, the majority of women who attended rituals were lesbian feminists. For those coming out of the consciousness raising groups of the late 1960s and early 1970s, the all-female environment for spiritual purposes was an easy stretch. Many lesbians, who already preferred and prioritized the company of women, were attracted by the emphasis on the bonds between women (Eller, 1995). Dianic tradition provided what Z described as "the only tradition that women could come to and attend to their own souls" (Budapest, personal communication), with no male god or male authority. It is a spiritual tradition that honors female sexuality free from male control, and provides a space where lesbians can celebrate and honor their sexuality as sacred. The fact that Dianic tradition seeks to reconcile feminist politics and religion into a feminist spirituality is a bridge that some women cannot cross, while others joyfully dance over. Noonan states that "Dianics, who meet in female-only covens and concentrate solely on the Goddess, are the most marked of the larger group of feminist witches: They are the 'radical feminists' of the spiritual feminist community" (1998, p. 2). Thirty years after

Z Budapest's first winter solstice ritual, women-identified women from all sexual orientations are still attracted to Dianic women-only ritual space, where lesbian feminist politics and concerns are often at the foundation of magical practice.

Some lesbian Dianic practitioners have a personal or political basis for purposefully excluding men in ritual. Z Budapest's early book, *The Feminist Book of Lights and Shadows*, ". . . defined feminist Witchcraft as Dianic" (Jade, 1991, p. 69). In *Manifesto of the Susan B. Anthony Coven #1*, Z Budapest writes;

> We are committed to teaching wimmin how to organize themselves as witches and to sharing our traditions with wimmin. We are opposed to teaching our magic and our craft to men. Our immediate goal is to congregate with each other according to our ancient woman-made laws and remember our past, renew our powers and affirm our Goddess of the Ten-thousand Names. (1976, p. 2)

According to Jade, "Although Z did not identify the Craft as a lesbian religion, she did identify it as a separatist tradition, and this promoted the concept of Dianic Wicca as 'the' religion of many lesbian separatists" (1991, p. 69).

For other lesbian Dianics, as well as heterosexual and bisexual Dianics, excluding males from participation in ritual is not born from a rejection of males but rather an embracing of women's unique biological rites of passage and how living in female body in a patriarchal world informs and effects our lives. Noonan states, "This separatism is seen as necessary for women in a patriarchal world, a religious 'room of one's own' in which to heal wounds inflicted by male-dominated society. . . ." (1988, pp. 153-154). Many women choose Dianic separatist ritual simply because of the joy, fun, pleasure, feeling of safety, and value which they derive from being in a exclusively female space with other like-minded women (Barrett, in press).

Representing a central mythic theme of woman-identified cosmology, Diana, the Roman Goddess of the Hunt, and name-giver of Dianic tradition, was known as Artemis by the Greeks. She is the protector of women and of the wild, untamed spirit of nature. While Diana does have a triple aspect, it is in Her aspect as Virgin Huntress that She guides Her daughters to wholeness. She is "virgin" in the ancient sense of "She Who Is Whole Unto Herself." The ancient meaning of "virgin" described a woman who was unmarried, autonomous, belonging solely to herself. The original meaning of this word was not attached to sexual act with a man. Diana/Artemis did not associate herself or consort with men, which is why these Goddesses are often understood to be lesbian. The Goddess Artemis or Diana (Dia Anna, meaning, "Nurturer Who

Does Not Bear Young") was the name that women would call for in childbirth labor since Artemis' mother experienced no pain in childbirth. Dianic women express an understanding of Diana/Artemis as the "spiritual warrior" and call Her forth from within themselves in their personal magical practice (Barrett, in press). She is the one who can focus Her will and direct energy to Her goals. In the early dawn of the feminist spirituality movement, the Goddess Diana became a role model for personal autonomy and feminist activism, protecting and defending women's right to live without fear. Lesbians identified with Her as a symbol of a strong, free, and capable woman walking in the world without fear and without the need of a male consort to be whole (Barrett, in press).

The spiritual and religious phenomenon of the return of the Goddess to human consciousness is a new and ancient paradigm of living in balance with one another and the Earth. Fundamental to feminist Goddess spirituality is the belief that women must work to heal the personal and political imbalances caused by the various manifestations of patriarchy that have dominated the Earth and humanity for the past 5,000 years.

The word "patriarchy" means "rule of the fathers," and describes the worldwide dominant political structures within which we live. I am going to use the word "patriarchy" to describe the institutionalized self-perpetuating political, religious, and economic system of dominance and subordination (Lerner, 1993) which has been linked to racism, sexism, class-ism, looks-ism, homophobia, violence against women and children, and destruction of nature (Griffin, 1978). Eisler describes patriarchy as a social system wherein ". . . the primary principle of social organization is ranking backed up by fear and/or force" (1995, p. 4). Patriarchy is a way of thinking that permeates our actions both consciously and unconsciously. It is the polluted water in which we all swim. Although men historically are, and have been, the primary perpetrators of patriarchy and continue to derive the greatest privilege from this imbalance of power, women and children also cannot help but swallow this water to greater or lesser degrees. Women and men alike are affected by patriarchal thinking, for it is inherent in the very fabric of our culture, the context of our lives. Patriarchy is the paradigm of our world, the filter through which we view and experience life as compartmentalized and disjointed, rather than whole and interdependent. Until we become aware that patriarchy is both an internal and external system, and work to heal ourselves from its effects, we will continue to think and act out of this patriarchal paradigm. Dianic ritual seeks a transformation in women's consciousness from patriarchal conditioning by restoring value to women's lives and validating an egalitarian worldview based on a respectful and harmonious relationship with nature.

From earliest times, across most cultures and religions, women have participated in ceremony that is gender based and separate (Cohen, 1991). Although some people use the words "ceremony" and "ritual" interchangeably, ceremony describes a series of acts, often symbolic, as prescribed by law, religion, or state. Ceremony generally implies little to no improvisation, and is generally more rote, regimented, and concerned with the exact order of actions and the precision of each enactment to mark the moment in time. On the other hand, the purpose of ritual is transformation. Although ritual is likely to have a specific purpose, structure, enactments, and direction of flow, its flexible form allows room to breathe and incorporates the unforeseen and unexpected inspirations and responses of the women facilitating and participating. Although there may be transformational aspects to ceremony and ceremonial aspects to ritual, the internal result of the experience indicates which form is dominant in the occasion: transformation or a marking of time.

To heal and change past attitudes and beliefs that influence the present, many women are creating rituals that revisit our own experiences and life milestones. There is healing in giving ourselves in the present what we were not able to give ourselves in the past. A post-menopausal woman might create or participate in a menarche ritual that may help to heal her from generations of familial denial of that important passage for young women. Countless times I have witnessed the power of ritual to transcend linear time and heal past pain.

Creating and participating in ritual brings value to any life passage, transition, or event that a woman finds personally significant or wishes to make significant, whether they are physical crossroads or emotional transitions. It is through women's rites that women can connect with and honor the deepest parts of their selves, bringing their inner knowledge to conscious awareness. It is also within ritual that women witness and support one another in their path of healing and diverse celebrations of the rites of life. The reclaiming and recreation of women's rites takes the diverse threads of women's lives and weaves them into a tapestry, a whole multicolored cloth of physical, emotional, and spiritual health. Ritual serves as a bridge to carry meaning to the personal or collective mind through the manipulation of symbolic objects, specific activities or actions. When ritual is purposefully created and enacted, women are transformed. The past, present, and future become linked in a continuum that can be observed, felt, and learned from. When life's passages are clearly marked through ritual, we can connect the dots of events in our lives to see the larger pattern in what may have previously felt like a random series of events. We can observe, understand, and integrate those events that have shaped our attitudes about womanhood, sexuality, love, and life.

In the aftermath of a significant transition, we formulate life decisions, consciously or unconsciously. We internalize these attitudes or beliefs about ourselves, our bodies, our sexuality and life in general based on how our life experiences are responded to, or not, by others and ourselves. These internalized decisions influence us in our present and continue to into our future, affecting our behavior, actions, and choices. Unexamined, negative subconscious decisions can have devastating and far-reaching effects.

An example of this would be a girl's first menstruation. Too often, this first experience is met with secrecy, embarrassment or shame. Somewhat more positively, but less frequently, the girl's parents do their best to not make it a "big deal." Internally, the girl develops an attitude that either being a woman is dirty or shameful, or becoming a woman is "no big deal." Either decision follows her into womanhood, affecting her relationship with her body, her sexuality and the physical symptoms of her monthly cycle. In other words, *what we do or don't do in treating or responding to a significant life passage or transition can have an enormous effect on the rest of that woman's life.*

According to medical intuitive and healer Caroline Myss, every memory, decision, and attitude has an energetic factor or consequence to it. There is an energetic "cost" to not dealing with these negative past or present experiences. For every negative experience we have had that has not been consciously dealt with, there continues to be a "leaking" of one's present life force energy to that past experience. Myss states that "You are in as many places as your emotional energy takes you," and that using your present reservoir of energy to "finance" the past is one of the causes for susceptibility to physical illness (Myss, 1996). Ritual provides an opportunity to address memories, decisions, and attitudes energetically. Myss states that "It is never too late to call your spirit back," and "unplug" your circuits from those experiences (Myss, 1996).

Unlike other religious and spiritual traditions where the religious tradition is deposited in an external source (Brown, 1995), Dianic ritual centers on the ritualizing of the female body where the healing and revelatory experiences are made possible through the unification of the body/mind. By incorporating intuitive movement, dancing, chanting, drumming, and sounding, meaning and healing can be achieved at a deep level, especially when accompanied by a clear intention of the ritual's purpose. Brown states that "Meaning is not in the world; it is not out there waiting to be found. Meaning is created in the interaction between the self and the other, the one and the many, the group and the natural world" (1995, p. 217). The spiritual experience is *embodied* in the women, and a fundamental intention of Dianic tradition can be realized: to re-sacralize the female body as manifestation of the Goddess, the Source from where all things emerge and return. Lesbians, who may have internalized homophobia as an extra layer of misogyny to heal from, can experience positive transformation by experiencing the benefits of a spiritual tradition that says the body of a woman who loves women is holy.

Through providing ritual facilitation for numerous personal rituals as well as large seasonal celebrations for over two decades, I have seen the power that ritual-making has for lesbians, and its transcendent healing effects. Lesbians have different rites of passage and significant occasions from heterosexual women's. Thus, it is imperative that lesbians create rituals that reflect our life experiences, make our lives visible to non-lesbians and, more importantly, to ourselves. Some rites specifically for lesbians might include a ritual honoring falling in love with a woman for the first time, or accepting oneself as a lesbian as in a "coming out" ritual. A ritual to honor one's choice to live as an "out" lesbian in the workplace, love-making rituals, union ceremonies, choosing to become a mother, or choosing not to birth a child, and rituals to heal from internalized homophobia would all be strengthening and empowering celebrations of lesbian life. Because of the power inherent in the medium of ritual, I have made my spiritual service about teaching ritual-making and facilitation skills to women. If we lesbians don't provide this for each other and ourselves who will?

The impact upon our lives as lesbians, from passages that were unmarked by ritual is impossible to fully comprehend. Many lesbians are creating rituals to help heal and change attitudes or beliefs that influence their present consciousness. They are magically reaching back into the past, revisiting experiences, making different decisions based on new awareness, and marking milestones that were not recognized as significant at the time.

I have included here brief descriptions of three rituals all related to lesbians: one for lesbians choosing to have children, one for a group of lesbians who chose not to have children and wanted to ritually honor that choice, and a group "coming-out" ritual. I assisted the recipients in the creation and facilitation of each of these described rituals (Barrett, in press).

RITUAL FOR ENTERING THE CIRCLE OF MOTHERS

In the cycle of women's mysteries, this ritual offers a tremendous opportunity for psychic and physical empowerment of the mothers-to-be. The baby shower, so customary for heterosexual women, has begun in recent years to become an expected ritual occasion for lesbian mothers. This ritual can be a meaningful experience, especially if entered into with a clear intention of what the moms hope to accomplish with it. The ritual planning begins by asking the birth mother and her partner, What are their needs? What does the birth mother hope to experience in giving birth? In parenting? What kind of verbal and hands-on support do they wish from their friends and family within the ritual itself?

In order of age, the invited women are admitted into the circle and anointed by Holly, a close friend of Lisa and Janet's, the mothers-to-be. Holly touches each woman's brow with seawater, representing the womb water of the Goddess, from where the spirit of all life emerges into form. Women join hands in one circle, and Holly invites the elemental powers to bless the mothers-to-be and the child Lisa contains in her womb.

To mark their rite of passage in to parenthood, Lisa and Janet wanted to create a symbolic delineation of this immanent change in their lives. At the couple's request, the circle separates into two smaller circles side by side. One circle consists of women who do not parent children, have not given birth to a child, or have chosen not to. The other contains a circle of women who parent children, have physically birthed children, and their partners. Lisa and Janet walk to the center of the first circle. One by one, the couple embraces the women in that circle and say farewell to the life they have known without the responsibilities of parenthood. Their friends acknowledge that the couple will be stepping through a door and will be forever changed. They all affirm that they will stay supportive and connected.

Holly escorts Lisa and Janet out of the first circle to the edge of the circle of mothers symbolizing the transition they have now begun. Lisa and Janet are welcomed into the circle of mothers, first by Lisa's own mother, or by a close motherly friend. Their bodies are blessed and decorated with red ochre, symbolic of the life giving blood of the womb.

The circles rejoin into one as the new mothers-to-be are honored and blessed by the entire circle. Holly takes a ball of red string and ties a bracelet around her left wrist. She passes the ball to the woman on her left, who ties the string around her left wrist. The ball of yarn is passed around the circle in this way until all the women are bound together by the strand of blood-red string. The group pauses to look around the circle, and acknowledge that they are united through the blood of their wombs. A scissors is passed, and each woman cuts the string that binds her to the woman on her left, leaving a bracelet on her wrist that she will continue to wear. The women focus their prayers for a safe and healthy birth. Holly instructs them to cut their string off and bury it with gratitude, after the child arrives. Lisa and Janet are presented with gifts with which to create a birthing altar to use as a focus before and during labor. The ritual gifts reflect Lisa as she embodies the Goddess who brings forth and sustains life in strength and love. The Goddess and the elements are thanked, and the circle is opened. After the sharing of food, additional gifts usually associated with the traditional baby shower for the care of the infant are presented to the moms.

HONORING THE CHOICE TO NOT HAVE CHILDREN

Patriarchal society emphasizes a woman's worth by birth giving. Lesbians and other women who choose not to have children often have to defend themselves to family, friends, and the culture at-large. Women who are childless by choice are judged as "selfish," "unfulfilled," "incomplete as a woman," "un-feminine," "unnatural," "must hate children," and a "disappointment" to their families. Women who choose not to give birth may feel invisible in conversations with other women where the unspoken expectation from birth to physical maturity is to have children. The Goddess in Her aspect as Mother, or Maker, She who Manifests, includes all women regardless of whether they have given birth to children or not, or whether her womb has been removed by hysterectomy. The womb of woman, or her womb space, still serves as the metaphorical, if not literal, symbol of woman's powerful creative potential, where ideas are birthed into form as art, music, writing, dance, and careers. A woman who chooses another primary way to manifest her creative power in the world needs to be honored for her choice, not condemned.

The group ritual begins with the women speaking aloud the internalized voices of culture: religion, parents, and her own self. Once all the words are spoken, they are written down, and the paper that contains them is burned, symbolically releasing each woman from the expectations of others. The ritual space is purified with herbs to clear the energy and make a transition space to honoring their choices. Cyndy speaks about the womb as the literal and symbolic source of potential and fertility that each woman has known. Her words honor their womb blood as creative power, to be channeled how they choose, and to reclaim their wombs as the "cauldron" of creation. Each woman blesses her womb, anointing her belly with scented oil. She says aloud what she has created, and how she sustains and protects her creations, how she "mothers." She has brought a symbol of her creativity to add to the altar. Each woman follows Cyndy's example and declares how she "uses her woman blood" to create beauty and meaning in her life, followed by a physical symbol of her creation. The ritual concludes with words that honor their choice, and all the many ways women use their creative energies.

COMING OUT AS A LESBIAN

To declare a lesbian identity can bring fear and distancing from others. By ritualizing this important transition, we create a cauldron of support that brings the newly out lesbian into communion with others.

Blessed be the fire of our desire.
Blessed be our courage.
Blessed be our love.

–Chant by Sue McGowan

The women gather at the lakeside to give themselves and one another a ritual they had previously never conceived able to experience; that of celebrating woman-loving women in the open, lesbian community, and honoring their path as amazons in the world. At the water's edge the elements are invoked and women then look toward the collection of driftwood that forms an opening to move through to the other side. Some women stand on the other side of the passage to welcome as a single drum beats to their breath. Each woman briefly tells the others of her awakening and process of coming out to her lesbian identity. At the threshold of the passage she is asked, "Who are you," and she responds, declaring herself, "I am Ruth, and I am a lesbian!" amid cheers of her sisters, until all the women are on the other side of the passage. A chant begins, "Blessed be the fire of our desire. Blessed be our courage. Blessed be our love," as women move into free-form dance to express their joy. A cauldron is lit to ceremonially ignite lesbian sacred sexuality, as women continue to dance and feed each other sweet mangos.

REFLECTION

Practitioners of Dianic tradition, lesbian and non-lesbian, actively work through personal and group ritual practices to vision and create a world where the web of life, which includes all living things, is honored as the sacred creation of the Goddess. While this article does not contain all the nuances of Dianic ritual, the ritual concepts and themes that have been incorporated into contemporary women's rituals for well over the past three decades were first made available by Dianic tradition, including union ceremonies for lesbians (Budapest, 1989). The values and practices of Dianic tradition have so deeply influenced and inspired the focus on lesbian and women-only ritual within the contemporary Goddess movement. For lesbians to honor our unique rites of passage that have been ignored or devalued by the dominant culture reflects a deep commitment to end patriarchal oppression both personally and globally. In naming and claiming our rites as lesbians, we restore meaning, value, and a sense of the sacred to our lives, the lives of our lovers, and loved ones.

REFERENCES

Adler, P., & Adler, P. (1987). *Membership roles in field research*. Thousand Oaks, CA: Sage.

Barrett, R. (in press). *Women's rites, women's mysteries: Creating personal and group ritual*.

Brown, K. (1995). Serving the spirits: The ritual economy of Haitian voodoo. In D. Cosentino (Ed.), *Sacred arts of Haitian voodoo* (pp. 216-218). Hong Kong: South Sea International Press.

Budapest, Z. (1976). *The feminist book of lights and shadows*. Luna Publications.

Budapest, Z. (1979). *The holy book of women's mysteries, vol. 1*. Los Angeles, CA: Susan B. Anthony Coven No. 1.

Budapest, Z. (1989). *The holy book of women's mysteries*. Berkeley: Wingbow.

Cohen, D. (Ed.). (1991). *The circle of life: Rituals from the human family album*. San Francisco: Harper San Francisco.

Daly, M. (1973). *Beyond God the father: Toward a philosophy of women's liberation*. Boston: Beacon Press.

Eisler, R. (1988). *The chalice and the blade: Our history, our future*. San Francisco: Harper.

Eisler, R. (1995). *Sacred pleasure*. Harper Collins: New York.

Eller, C. (1995). *Living in the lap of the goddess: The feminist spirituality movement in America*. Boston: Beacon Press.

Eller, C. (2000). The roots of feminist spirituality. In W. Griffin (Ed.), *Daughters of the goddess* (pp. 35). Walnut Creek, CA: Alta Mira Press.

Gimbutas, M. (1974). *The gods and goddesses of Old Europe: 7000 to 3500 b.c. myths, legends and cult images*. Berkley: University of California Press.

Gimbutas, M. (1989). *The language of the goddess*. San Francisco: Harper & Row.

Griffin, S. (1978). *Woman and nature*. New York: Harper & Row.

Griffin, W. (Ed.) (2000). *Daughters of the goddess: Studies of healing, identity and empowerment*. Walnut Creek, CA: AltaMira Press.

Griffin, W. (in press). Returning to the mother of us all. In S. Arvind & K. Young (Eds.), *Through her eyes: Women's perspectives on world religions*. Boulder, CO: Westview Press.

Hutton, R. (1999). *The triumph of the moon*. New York: Oxford University Press.

Jade. (1991). *To know*. Oak Park, IL: Delphi Press.

Lerner, G. (1993). *The creation of feminist consciousness* (pp. 3-6). New York: Oxford University Press.

Mountainwater, S. (1991). *Ariadne's thread*. Freedom, CA: Crossing Press.

Myss, C. (1996). *Energy anatomy*. Boulder, CO: Sounds True Recordings.

Noonan, K. (1998). May you never hunger: Religious foodways in Dianic witchcraft. *Ethnologies, 20*(1-2), 151-173.

Sjoor, M., & Mor, B. (1987). *The great cosmic mother: Rediscovering the religion of the earth*. San Francisco: Harper.

Starhawk. (1979). *The spiral dance: A rebirth of the ancient religion of the Great Goddess*. New York: Harper and Row.

Stone, M. (1976). *When God was a woman*. New York: Dial Press.

RESOURCES

Temple of Diana, Inc.

Dianic classes, workshops, and rituals The Spiral Door Women's Mysteries School of Magick and Ritual Arts, a Dianic clergy training program with Ruth Barrett and Falcon River, P.O. Box 6425, Madison, WI 53716 (608) 226-9998

chngemkers@aol.com

www.templeofdiana.org

Z Budapest
Women's Spirituality Forum, workshops, readings, conferences
www.zbudapest.com

Reformed Congregation of the Goddess
International Networking, conferences for Goddess women
P.O. Box 6530, Madison, WI 53716
(608) 226-9998
rcgi@itis.com
www.goddesswomen.com

Circle of Aradia/Reformed Congregation of the Goddess, Inc.
Dianic seasonal rituals, ongoing classes, special events
P.O. Box 461630, Los Angeles, CA 90046
(323) 650-1605

Ritual Encounters of the Queer Kind:
A Political Analysis
of Jewish Lesbian Ritual Innovation

Marla Brettschneider

SUMMARY. Jewish feminist and queer engagement in Jewish life and Judaism are transforming the practices and foundational orientations of traditional modes. Jewish feminist, queer ritual innovation in particular is inspired by an array of secular and radical critical theories as much as it is by the historic concrete experiences of a diversity of Jews in different Jewish communities. It is important to hold all of us who are involved in religious ritual innovation responsible to the knowledges we have developed and learned in critical theory or we risk, even with the best of intentions and creativity, re-inscribing some of the very problems of traditional ontological norms that we might have originally sought to disrupt and subvert. This article looks specifically at examples of new "coming out" rituals for Jewish queers explored over time in the Jewish Queer Think Tank: honoring them as well as offering tools from secular critical theory to assist our work in keeping them accountable to our aspirations to both love and fundamentally transform Jewishness. Here I redefine the function of religious ritual itself in political terms as an identity-producing

---

Marla Brettschneider is Associate Professor of political philosophy at the University of New Hampshire, with a joint appointment in Political Science and Women's Studies.

Address correspondence to: Dr. Marla Brettschneider, 318 Horton, University of New Hampshire, Durham, NH, 03824 (E-mail: marlab@cisunix.unh.edu).

[Haworth co-indexing entry note]: "Ritual Encounters of the Queer Kind: A Political Analysis of Jewish Lesbian Ritual Innovation." Brettschneider, Marla. Co-published simultaneously in *Journal of Lesbian Studies* (Harrington Park Press, an imprint of The Haworth Press, Inc.) Vol. 7, No. 2, 2003, pp. 29-48; and: *Lesbian Rites: Symbolic Acts and the Power of Community* (ed: Ramona Faith Oswald) Harrington Park Press, an imprint of The Haworth Press, Inc., 2003, pp. 29-48. Single or multiple copies of this article are available for a fee from The Haworth Document Delivery Service [1-800-HAWORTH, 9:00 a.m. - 5:00 p.m. (EST). E-mail address: docdelivery@haworthpress.com].

performance. As such I utilize social constructionist queer theories (i.e., Shane Phelan and Judith Butler), anarchists (i.e., Emma Goldman), and those involved in radical theatre (i.e., Augusto Boal) to articulate the revolutionary potential of ritual innovation. *[Article copies available for a fee from The Haworth Document Delivery Service: 1-800-HAWORTH. E-mail address: <docdelivery@haworthpress.com> Website: <http://www.HaworthPress.com>*

KEYWORDS. Ritual, lesbian, anarchy, queer theory, Jewish

In this paper I seek to bring the quite intellectual pursuit of philosophy into play with the not-necessarily-so-rational aspirations at work in many people's spiritual needs. For this project I hope to honor spiritual strivings while still holding them responsible for their political and theoretical merit. To do so I propose staging an encounter between Jewish lesbian interests in feminist ritual innovation, particular revolutionary thinkers/activists, and certain currents in lesbian and queer theory popular in the secular academy. Specifically, I examine an example of an idea for a Jewish coming out ritual discussed over time in the Jewish Queer Think Tank. Using the contributions of contemporary lesbian, queer, and other radical theorists I attempt to articulate one possible function of ritual as identity producing, revolutionary performance.

In the following pages I will argue that by using the work of Shane Phelan we can avoid the essentialist presumptions of lesbian identity common in U.S. secular culture encoded in the language of "coming out." Once we establish queer identity as a social construction in need of constant reconstitution, we can make use of the anarchist notion of preparation for determining the role of ritual in such reconstitutions. In this context we will examine Augusto Boal's contributions on the political potential of theatre to enable certain self-conscious reconstitutions. If we think of ritual as a kind of theatre, we can take seriously the roles of participants as actors in a ritual performance. To clarify the radical possibilities in this move, I utilize Judith Butler's theory of performativity where sex, gender, and sexuality are not understood as inherent traits but as identities produced through their very enactments. In sum, I will argue that lesbian and queer theory, along with the help of certain core anarchist concepts and Boal's projects in radical theatre, can be employed in feminist-situated and lesbian/queer Jewish ritual innovation. The goal here is to keep our spiritual journeys grounded in, rather than serving as a refuge or flight from, politics. In this way I suggest bridging an all-too-common secular-spiritual divide in the service of the democratic pursuit of making possible what seems impossible about our radical visions and aspirations.

JEWISH QUEER INNOVATIONS: A COMING OUT RITUAL?

For those doing Jewish lesbian and feminist ritual innovation, it is clear that their lesbianism and feminism inform their engagement with their Jewishness. I think, however, that the "sense" in which this "informing" works has thus far been under-theorized communally. Thus, even for those involved in lesbian and feminist ritual innovation, the "stuff" of intense critical lesbian and feminist theory often remains too separated from the ritual engagement. I want to think here about the "encounter" of critical theory and spirituality more explicitly.

I am privileged to serve as the coordinator of a group, called by its members the "Jewish Queer Think Tank" (JQTT), that was originally formed as a project of JAGL (Jewish Activist Gays and Lesbians–a New York City-based political activist group). The JQTT meets quarterly to examine issues of concern to Jewish sexual minorities in the context of both the larger queer and Jewish communities. After about four years of meeting together, some members brought up the issue of queer Jewish rituals. Eventually, the group responded to the call of one member, T., to create a "coming out ritual." This member's desire, and the group's affirmative response, for such a ritual may be seen as part of a growing awareness and movement on the part of feminists and queers to address aspects of our lives, relationships, and life paths that need to be acknowledged, marked, celebrated, and explored spiritually–or recognized publicly as sacred–that have been left out of Jewish practice historically framed by elite Jewish men.

Jewish elite men have rituals that mark moments on a life path that they have experienced as important: circumcision, marriage, death, etc. Feminists have noted that any number of experiences that may be considered important historically for many women (for example: first menstruation, first girlfriend, childbirth, miscarriage, becoming a senior, divorce and other separations, etc.) have gone unnoticed in the ritual cycle of elite male-defined Jewish communal life. Feminists have begun to create new, and adapt old, rituals to bring the sacred into the cycles of their bodily and collective lives and/or to make sacred the significant moments of their life paths. With the expansion of rituals stimulated by Jewish feminists, we increasingly find queers exploring similar terrain.[2]

It is probably no coincidence that one of the first places a self-defined queer Jewish group might begin its exploration of rituals would be related to the notion of "coming out." In contemporary U.S. culture, what has been identified as the coming out experience has been foregrounded as the central defining moment in the lives of people who consider themselves GLBTQ. Many people came out under extremely difficult, if not life-threatening, circumstances. For many, it has been the most pivotal experience in their lives. In the absence of any existent ritual in traditional Judaism to accompany such an event, it is understandable that some Jews might want one. Without communal affirmation, this intense experience often isolates many individual queer Jews from Jewish community. We also increasingly hear of Jewish feminists and queers envisioning the power of ritual adaptation to address individual and communal needs as well as current and historical yearnings for repair, rejuvenation, justice, redemption.

T. imagined a ceremony where people who had come out in a given year would be welcomed by those already out. This vision turned the homophobic push to isolate and pathologize gayness on its head. Further, in the Jewish mystical tradition, liminal moments are understood as inherently powerful; they are both dangerous and imbued with transformative potential. T. recognized coming out as a liminal time and sought to address the discomfort that liminality often stirs without normalizing the experience. To achieve this, we looked to the communal aspect of Jewish ritual, utilizing the cross-generational and cross-gender make-up of Jewish queer community. The diversity inherent in any particular Jewish community can serve queer needs. For example, seeing ourselves across a spectrum of age, gender, circumstance, and positionality within Jewish queer community reminds us that we are all in process. It also opens possibilities for mentoring across difference as role models and mentors play significant roles particularly for minorities within any given community.

Coming out has often been described as a "finding oneself," "coming home," or "finding one's community." And yet, many queers coming out experience, or fear, excommunication from community and/or being turned out of the home. If we were to ritualize the coming out experience in a communal (rather than individual/private) way, we might work to problematize this dynamic in which many people feel acceptance and exclusion simultaneously. How do we utilize ritual to address and transform this phenomenon? As an act of empowerment, we in the JQTT asked specifically: What could a ritual of "welcome" look like? In the JQTT discussions we explored images in Jewish tradition and the Hebrew word for welcome: *Brucha Haba'a* (blessed is the one who comes). Ironically, although coming (*ba*) might not have a queer or otherwise sexual connotation in Hebrew, we find that the very word for welcoming when translated into English has multiple meanings for queer Jews in the U.S. A Jewish queer "welcoming" ritual in the specificity of a Jewish language and tradition can serve to welcome as it suggests making sacred coming out and the pleasures of sexuality for U.S. queer Jews.

The JQTT thought the event could be a welcoming ritual, with words and Hebrew songs of blessing. We discussed moving into a circle formed by those already out embracing a smaller circle comprised of the newly out in our community. For a moment in time the newly out would experience looking out to a world populated by loving, accepting people. The ritual creates a time/space to see a world of mentors, path breakers, communally engaged queers in relation. The time/space of the ritual disrupts the other time/spaces in which the newly out all too often face hostility, incomprehension, isolation.

The discussion and the play of images at the JQTT meetings were sincere and heartfelt. We were engaging with Jewish tradition and history, exploring aspects that have come down to us in our place and time as empowering, and those aspects that have been used in, or as justifications for, the oppression of women and queers. For example, T. offered the imagery of the "living waters" of the *mikvah* in Jewish tradition that could be reclaimed to symbolize "the fullness of life after the death of the closet." Traditionally this ritual was used to cleanse the soul and prepare the body for the holiness of such experiences as the Sabbath or sexual relations. As one example, observant women must go to the mikvah after their menses and the ritual is a requirement before their husbands will have sex with them again (following the period of sexual abstinence Jewish tradition has developed during a wife's menses). Many women have found this ritual very spiritual. The mikvah and its imagery has also often been deployed in the Jewish patriarchal control of women's bodies and their (presumed hetero)sexuality. We thought we could reclaim mikvah and its symbolism and reconnect it with our sexuality in new ways.

Before further exploration of mikvah and other rituals, however, we need to address certain more theoretical aspects of the phenomena. From our work together in the JQTT over the course of more than a year, it became clear to me that we need new rituals as part of the transformation of Jewish life as well as part of disrupting the notion that heterosexuality is normative. But we must also be careful about how we construct these new rituals, whether they be related to mikvah or any other aspect of Jewish tradition. We must ask deep questions regarding just what sorts of ritual innovations will, in fact, be disruptive of heterosexual normativity. We must be cautious not to replace traditional essentialist notions with new ones. In this spirit, I want to subject the very notion of a coming out ritual to critical inquiry.

CREATIVE JEWISH QUEER RITUALS:
THE CHALLENGE OF (BE)COMING OUT

A coming out ritual may serve as part of a wider project to end hetero-sexism. Depending on the context, however, a coming out ritual may also risk reinforcing a number of problematic ideas about, and practices involved in, queer lives. As Phelan (1994) points out, the notion of "coming out" has tended to presuppose an inner, or inherent, essence of gayness. Much of the narrative of coming out presumes that being gay "is" uncontestedly a part of some human beings. This understanding is grounded in a view that being gay is an ahistorical phenomena, an individual essence. As many queer theorists have discussed, however, being gay is historically situated and culturally con-structed. In an effort to challenge the potential essentialism in the coming out narrative, Phelan writes that coming out as gay is, instead, a process of (be)coming out. It is not simply the expression of an *a priori* state or orienta-tion, formerly hidden and now exposed. Rather, coming out is a process of "creating oneself" as gay. Over time, in a combination of individually and col-lectively situated processes, we create queer culture, cultivate new epis-temologies, interact with heterosexual and heterosexist societies in myriad ways developing our very identities as lesbians and queers.

What happens when we submit ritual innovations to such philosophical critique and how can Phelan's insights assist us in critiquing the welcoming ritual discussed above? Are there ways to tap into the welcoming kernel of that ritual that do not play into hegemonic understandings about identity? Can we think about a coming out ritual that does not reinforce an essentialist, ahistorical notion of homosexuality? How can we have a ritual that brings the power and empowerment of the sacred and of community to the process of be-coming out? What kinds of imagery could such a be-coming out ritual employ?

First, Phelan's contribution enables us to discard a strict dichotomy be-tween those "coming out" and those "out." That in a particular ritual there can be a circle clearly composed of "those out" and one of those only now coming out seems less possible and less attractive if we take into account the complex-ity of our lives as queers, the continual processes of be-coming out and conjur-ing our queer selves and communities. In naming the cloudiness of the once clear "out" and "newly out" distinction, it is not that we should suppose that everyone is the same. However, if coming out is a be-coming out, then every-one is always in the process of constructing their sexualities. This suggests that everyone is always be-coming out even as we are all likely to be doing so rather differently, have been consciously doing so for longer or shorter spans of time, attaching different significances to it, prioritizing it differently, etc.

Some of us never felt the experience of "coming out" sexually at all, though most of us face challenges everyday regarding coming out, being out, and all manner of be-comings. For many lesbians, relating to other women sexually was a gradual process involved in our becoming feminists and living and working within feminist communities. Yet even for these lesbians, setting up bank accounts, holding hands while out for a walk, or demanding family status in hospital visits all require decisions of be-coming out. In noting that we are always in a be-coming out process, is there still a way to honor the needs of those to whom this process seems newer?

Second, Phelan's concept that we are all always in the process of be-coming out suggests that there is not some fixed group to be welcomed into. There is, instead, a group–of individuals in different manners and in different phases of–constructing themselves as queer and constructing queer communities. How does this insight transpose the concept of welcoming altogether? Who needs welcoming in this case? By whom? For what? Is it also possible to see different groups with shifting memberships during the course of a ritual? The new questions of "who, by whom, and for what" may need to be answered in multiple ways. One's identity and role are likely to morph as the ritual unfolds and we can create a coming out ritual that is more democratic and multivocal (instead of fixed and identity bound).

A concrete example may be found in another coming out ritual explored within the JQTT. Originally unrelated to the JQTT's work, the New Jersey Gay and Lesbian Havurah developed a Coming Out Ritual for its own community. Some of the members then utilized their Havurah experience to do workshops with other queer Jewish groups. One member, David Rogoff, also did a workshop with their ritual at the Conference of the International Association of Gay and Lesbian Jews and eventually brought materials to the JQTT discussions.

The NJ G&LH's Coming Out Ritual is a beautiful collective piece of work in ongoing adaptation. It is sensitive, artistic, and performance oriented. The ritual draws deeply on Jewish history and liturgy, reclaimed in creative and moving ways, grounded in diversity within contemporary Jewish queer lives. Moreover, it manages to exemplify Phelan's conception of coming out as a be-coming out. The central portion of the ritual involves a series of shifting locations, transformations of the tradition in the service of queer Jewish experiences that acknowledge the many facets of coming out and the process-like manner of be-coming throughout one's lifetime. There are sections devoted to "coming out to ourselves," "coming out to family and friends," "coming out at work," "becoming involved in the gay community," "coming out in the Jewish community," and "coming out in the larger world." Through combined choreography and newly created blessings, it is clear that each section will be comprised of different subgroups of participants. Also, the ritual includes a mournful yet encouraging section dealing with "hope for those still in the closet."

In the JQTT we also spoke with David about the ways that such be-comings do not usually occur in any one or linear way. The different aspects of coming outs enable individuals and communities to work on new challenges for them over time. There can be no "culminating" point in the process of be-coming out, no "final" sphere to conquer. Similarly, the "hope for those still in the closet" needs to involve all of us in constantly pushing ourselves and drawing others further out of the closet. The notion of be-coming out breaks down the simple dichotomy of those closeted and those not. These insights may be helpful for other versions of be-coming out rituals. Even when multiple sites of coming-outs are incorporated, there can still be a tendency to employ a linear imaginary, symbolizing coming out as a process that follows a particular path and "ends" with a section suggesting "now you are out" (as if to say that "now your identity/community/justice-building work is done").

Let us explore another example of a ritual in order to push this point further. Visualize a group of people in a circle, each with their arms clasped around another's waist to make a strong barrier. In the center of the circle there are persons newly "coming out." They are asked to loosen up and move around the circle bumping into the people making the circle. Those forming the circle are singing songs with a quick, tense tempo. Those inside cannot get out; they come to feel stuck, closed in. At the prompting of the ritual facilitator, those making the circle change the shape of the ring forming two lines to suggest a pathway. The lines curve and shift. Those inside begin to walk through the path. The singing changes to cacophony. There are many songs at once: sad, up-beat, poignant, nostalgic, newly written for the event, funny, prayers, children's ditties. As the people walk through, the singing changes again to more harmonized-rhythmic chanting. Those at the back of the path run forward to keep it spreading out, twisting and turning. After some time, the facilitator prompts those making the path to stop elongating it. This allows the walkers to "emerge" from the path, at which point all are called to sing and dance together. The singing becomes jubilant with many voices singing together.

This ritual is intense and moving. The music sets mood, evoke experiences and emotions. At its onset, those newly out recall the trapped feeling of being in the closet. The walk's beginning suggests the confusion many people feel when first coming out. The road shifts in unexpected ways but we grow more familiar with our surroundings, developing relationships, and building coping, resistance, and survival skills. Participants build momentum and finally emerge, "come out." The others now join them. The experience is cathartic and participants feel exalted. All sing and dance joyously like at any *simcha*, happy occasion.

Think how this ritual also relies on linear imagery of identity formation, as the finale occurs when the individuals are "out." Think how clearly it distinguishes between those who are in the closest/newly coming out, and those who are already out. The ending of the ritual homogenizes queer identity, mixing everyone together as if they are now all the same. And yet the twisting pathway suggests that the way is not simply linear. Occasionally some people forming the lines of the path may choose to run through path as well. Some who had been inside the circle may come to feel empowered to hold up part of the communal path. The ritual's last portion can change from all dancing together to traditional Jewish circle dances. The facilitator can call different individuals and groups into the center and back out to the communal circle, acknowledging the multiple sub-communities beyond "the newly out and the already out."

There are, will be, and need to be many "be-coming out" rituals that work for different individuals and diverse groups in changing contexts. There are likely to be many empowering aspects of any one ritual, and many opportunities to reassess a group's needs, rethink the implications of imagery employed, and redesign the rituals. These rituals can be a time to focus on the creative, constructionist, contingent, and fluid nature of queer sexualities. They can be a time to play collectively with the dialectic of meaning, community, risk, expression, sex, desire, passion, gender, sexuality, and power that is both operative and also impossibly possible. These musings bring us to some deeper questions regarding the very function of ritual. Ritual, important in the spiritual life of individuals and communities, can also be understood as fundamentally political. As part of the development of lesbian Jewish rituals, we may be able to understand ritual more broadly as a clear and directed aspect of revolutionary social change.

A POLITICAL FUNCTION OF RITUAL: ANARCHIST PREPARATION

Religious participation is often criticized for taking up the space of political activism within an oppressive social system. But is this necessarily so? Can religion, spirituality, searches for the sacred, and ritual be a part of political change? How might we think of ritual as, rather than a practice reinforcing the status quo, an aspect of social transformation? Without serious attention to such questions Jewish queer and other modes of ritual innovation run the risk of confining the very set of experiences they seek to liberate. In order to answer these questions I propose looking to the anarchist notion of preparation.

Orthodox Marxists/Leninists have traditionally prioritized activity that would bring about a whole scale revolution. Many have understood this revolution as existing within a bounded period of time. In this understanding, there is: a pre-revolutionary period, the revolution, and a post-revolutionary time. The function of the revolution is to radically alter the social relations in a given society. As such, it is speculated that the post-revolutionary time will be one in which social relations are then equal and democratic. Anarchists have their own version of this concept of revolution. They generally work with socialists, communists, and others toward *the* revolution. They do, however, place more emphasis on the relationships between the means of bringing about such a revolution and its ends.

Turning orthodox Marxist-Leninism on its head, anarchists suggest that the notion of a quick, sudden revolution should not necessarily be the exclusive focus for a revolutionary.[3] Certainly, we need a fundamental transformation, but we also desperately need to *prepare* ourselves for living democratically. Experiences of, and experiments with, social relations different from those at present enable us to live these alternative social relations as they become more possible on a grander scale, or in more localized contexts.[4] Engaging in the work of preparation, we learn how to practice democracy.[5] Significantly, we also often learn that there are mistakes or lapses in our visions that only living them out can show us. Participating in small scale, radically democratic projects empowers us *now* for our ongoing work. Taking on the tasks of egalitarian relationships and production now (without waiting for *the* revolution) allows us to explore the possible in the impossible structures of our current social relations.

One of the more inspiring and concise discussions on reinterpreting the (im)possible can be found in Emma Goldman's writings. In response to critiques of anarchism as "impractical, though a beautiful ideal," Goldman (1969) references playwright Oscar Wilde:

> A practical scheme . . . is either one already in existence, or a scheme that could be carried out under the existing conditions; but it is exactly the existing conditions that one objects to, and any scheme that could accept these conditions is wrong and foolish. The true criterion of the practical, therefore, is not whether the latter can keep intact the wrong and foolish; rather it is whether a scheme has vitality enough to leave the stagnant waters of the old, and build, as well as sustain, new life. (p. 49)

Wilde and Goldman see how accepting what is said to be "the" reality before us stifles us with impossibilities. These radicals of the theatre world have vision enough to see multiple realities, even those that are yet to be created, transforming the impossible into the very possible.

When anarchists and small communitarian socialists (e.g., the kibbutz movement in Israel) have discussed preparation as part of the strategy for making possible the impossible, they have usually used the examples of syndicated labour movements, learning cooperatives, worker-run factories and business, and/or small scale egalitarian communes. What I would like to suggest here is that ritual can also be a form of preparation. Through play, imagination, and accessing spiritual dimensions we create micro realities in ritual. If our visions of fundamental social transformation remain in the more orthodox Marxist/Leninist mode, we are likely to foreclose possibilities for change which ritual innovation is designed to open up. Thus, the anarchist perspective becomes more helpful for those interested in creative ritual development.

Let us now examine how anarchism might effect be-coming out rituals. The processes of "coming out" referred to here as "be-coming out" are part of a revolutionary process of disrupting heteronormativity and making possible queer lives. A Marxist/Leninist vision of queer revolution throws us back into a more stylized and static "coming out" phenomenon with a closeted time, the explosive moment of coming out, and then a life as out. This linear view bypasses the process and constructionist layers discussed above. The anarchist processes of experiments in radical democracy and alternative social relations over time allows for the complex, temporally shifting and constructionist view of queer life, much like Phelan's be-coming. In be-coming out we acknowledge that there are many modes of possible queerness and "outness," more than we might even be able to imagine in our current historical context. The anarchist view encourages us to keep working at opening possibilities.

Rituals that situate a clearly demarcated group of "out" queers welcoming a separate and clearly demarcated coming out group are likely to reinscribe the linear notion of coming out and to reinforce static identities. Exploring the radical potential in the anarchist view of revolution which acknowledges the uneven, often circular, messy realities of be-coming more egalitarian can therefore be important to those involved in Jewish queer and other forms of ritual innovation. In anarchist fashion, M., another JQTT member, described ritual as not only created to occur in a given time and space, but also about "imbuing action[s] and object[s] with intention and meaning." By ritualizing the ordinary, and not only the extraordinary such as the Marxist/Leninist revolutionary moment, we can transform the micro-politics of domination. Resonating with anarchist notions of spontaneity, such Jewish queer ritual innovation can play with the empowering potential of more flexible and less contrived modes of ritual.

There are many ways to ritualize mundane moments that make sense in the context of queer Jewish lives. For example, it is a common Jewish practice to put a *mezuzah* on our doorposts. The mezuzah establishes identity, community, and our spirituality of connectedness. Physically, a mezuzah is a small case hung diagonally in a door jamb, which includes a scroll with the words of a central prayer referred to as the *shma*. The shma asks us to identify that which we know to be our god, our most sacred knowledges. With this knowledge we are commanded to pay attention to all comings and goings, to love what we know as our god with all of our heart, all of our might, and all of our soul. We are called upon to carry our knowledge through the generations. Often observant Jews will reach up to touch a mezuzah in a doorway as they walk through it, and then kiss their fingers. The mezuzah helps make conscious for us moments of liminality, of crossings-through. Can we queer this idea? Can we utilize the practices involved with the mezuzah to infuse aspects of our queer mundane lives with the power of the sacred?

What knowledges do we want to be in touch with as we move through the locations in which we are more and less out, where we work on different aspects of the struggle to end anti-Semitism, homophobia, and all intersecting oppressions? Could we imagine mezuzot on all doorposts in queer places we go and in the various arenas of our daily lives? We could reach, or look, up to our imagined mezuzot when we need to focus as we walk into a hostile meeting, into a dance club in which we want to enjoy *and* do not want to make poor choices, into a family gathering which might be unaccepting. We can transform the traditional act of kissing the mezuzah into a way to stay aware of our own knowledge of righteousness, to remind us to keep our heart, minds, and arms open, to stay aware of when we need to protect ourselves.

We can transform a traditional practice to foster intention in our lives, as we attend to our relations in the world, in our work of social transformation. As anarchism suggests, the transformative potential of rituals can be found in micro-practices, in performing acts that help us keep our eye on the prize in trying situations. Whether it be in communal and elaborate rituals or individualized acts that we imbue with the sacred, let us take our cue from the theatrical experiences of Goldman and Wilde. In any number of motions, actions, roles, and performances, ritual may therefore also be seen as a form of political theatre. To clarify this concept, let us turn to a discussion of the work of Augusto Boal.

RITUAL AND THE TRADITION OF POLITICAL THEATRE

Augusto Boal is a Brazilian radical and performance artist. Developing theatre in the tradition of Brecht,[6] Boal understands drama as a specific tool in revolutionary praxis. Theatre, like religion, has often been seen as an escape from reality in such a way that diffuses potential political energy on the part of the oppressed. Boal and others seek to transform the cathartic tendencies in theatre into direct action. In his work, Boal often refers to theatre as the rehearsal for the revolution. In guerilla theatre, role playing, forum theatre, the joker system, and other imaginative theatre exercises those involved in a theatre of the oppressed use actors, ordinary people, setting, and style to enhance people's capacity to see the contradictions of the hierarchical systems in which we live. These dramaturgical techniques hone people's critical capacities and their imaginative potential. Through the exercises, happenings, and events people become actors, political actors. Within and from the theatrical projects people take action on the issues confronting their lives and the lives of their communities.

What does this have to do with the encounter between queer strivings for spiritual fulfillment and expression, and an exquisitely cynical or in many ways post-modern queer theory? Regarding Boal's notion that theatre is a rehearsal for the revolution, a post-modernist might critique Boal's retention of revolution as too modernist, stuck in a totalizing paradigm.[7] This is a significant critique. Perhaps another way to see this, however, is that Boal is too humble. Perhaps, the rehearsal for the revolution which Boal sees in radical theatre is part of unfolding revolutionary aspirations itself, as we examined above among anarchists. Invoking Langston Hughes within an anarchist tradition, we might say that the radical transformation of society need not be deferred.

One of the main strengths of Boal's work is how it engages ordinary people in some of the most radical forms of direct action. Experiments with political theatre also enhance these people's capacities to act individually and collectively in changing their life circumstances. Situating this work within the anarchist tradition, let us address the phenomenon that there is not some post-revolutionary moment which looks so different from now. There will not be a post-revolutionary time that a theorist or practitioner can predict prior to living out the processes involved in the radical transformations. Boal's theatre techniques are developed to encourage dialogue, feedback, problem solving, and self-critical examination. These are necessary in the difficult processes of social transformation. Similar to the anarchist notion of preparation, Boal writes that "only out of constant practice will the new theory arise" (1985, p. 79). Working with Boal's techniques, we come to see that the experiment with alterity is likely to be what alterity is. Alternative social relations are not some thing that we know not of now, but experimentation and play with alterity is the experience of alterity itself. To put it another way, there is not some "real" reality outside the theatre.[8]

Interestingly, in Boal's work we can see aspects of the various concerns thus far discussed in this article. For example, as a political activist, Boal discusses the spiritual nature of his work. In his view, new modes of theatre are necessary for the democratic imperative to help free our spirits and spiritual impulses.

Through Boal's work we can appreciate both the rituals of theatrical development and the theatrical elements of ritual. His art challenges the reality of what generally is considered the "real" and the unreality of that which is fictional and/or not yet real. He recognizes that a central limitation of what we tend to call reality is that it is confined to what is "supposedly already known" (1985, p. 76). In his theatre, reality is about creating what seems impossible, about opening up the unknown, the untried, the unexamined, and the unexplored. Finally, bringing us back to Phelan, he explores what it means for theatre to be "change and not a simple presentation of what exists: it is becoming and not being" (1985, p. 29). In the context of the anarchist idea of preparation and Boal's work in political theatre, we can now see that this is also where queer theory has much to offer queer Jews and all those interested in radical ritual innovation.

RITUAL INNOVATION AND PERFORMATIVITY IN QUEER THEORY

Boal is a player, an actor, creating a stage, a theatre of our mundane existing locations. He and his troupes enact dramaturgically to expose the contradictions of systems of exploitation. Working in every day settings jump-starts ordinary people out of the taken-for-grantedness of even their most minute social relations. Boal's players purposely make what seems to be normal no longer so. It is only a small step from here to Judith Butler's notion of performativity.[9]

Butler argues that the self is a social construction and that, therefore, every identity is a performance. In contrast to notions of the eternal Jewish self, for example, this theory suggests that Jews are those who perform Jewishness. To give a concrete example, Jews are not *expressing* our identity as Jews when we wear a Jewish star, presupposing some essential Jewishness about us that is now publically revealed. Instead, wearing a Jewish star is a performance of Jewishness. Wearing a Jewish star is the very act, repeated by many and part of myriad related acts, that creates a Jewish identity. Jews are people that ritualize moving through doorposts; Jews are people who put up and kiss mezuzot. Queer Jews might reclaim these performances in the process of living queer lives and ending heterosexist oppression. In Nietzschean fashion, Butler's assertion that there is no "'doer' behind the deed" (1999, p. 33) suggests for us that there is no Jew who puts on a Jewish star or kisses a mezuzah, a doer who acts out Jewishness. Instead, it is the acts themselves which constitute the (queer) Jew. What does this mean for ritual?

Boal writes that "theatre is action" (1985, p. 155) and has developed "theatre as politics, not just political theatre" (2001, p. 336). In related fashion, rather than seeing a performance as "about" life, Butler helps us to see that life is the performance. Concomitantly, ritual is not about creating a space outside of life or society. Life in society is itself a performance. Ritual may be used as a (somewhat) conscious alternative performance, as the Jewish queer imaginary mezuzah serves to enhance our intentionality. For Butler a subversive form of parody is one that does not stay on the level of parodying an original, but one that is a parody of "the very notion of" originals (1999, p. 175). Similarly, the JQTT discussed what sorts of ritual performances expose supposedly "non-ritual" acts as performances as well.[10] Shoring oneself up as s/he walks through the door, the cowboy, the observant Jew, the coquette enact a ritual of preparing themselves, their identities, strengths, and weaknesses at that moment at which they walk into a room. What might be the radical potential of breaking down the distinction between rituals as theatrical and the rest of life as "real?" In the queer-appropriation of kissing the mezuzah, a Jewish sexual outlaw grows confident in the face a difficult situation, making what might have previously been an impossible stance of courage now very possible. Alternatively, if in a communal ritual the participants act as empowered selves, this is not merely a quaint skit. A ritual which involves participants acting as empowered is a performance as "real" as all the disempowered performances the actors play everyday. We may have learned to be disempowered selves by being taught, expected, forced to act as disempowered selves over time. Similarly, as part of the revolutionary process we can in part learn to be empowered selves by acting as empowered selves. Like any revolution, in an anarchist understanding this doesn't happen suddenly and fully. We need practice. We need to pass through many doorways, finding many imaginary mezuzot as we prepare ourselves for a different world of social relations. Specific acts in which we play the roles of empowered selves, specific rituals that create opportunities for us to engage with ourselves and others as empowered selves, are some of the many excellent modes of "preparation" for living more fully as empowered selves within and beyond a ritualized experience.

RITUAL, REVOLUTION, PERFORMANCE: ISSUES OF REPETITION

Butler (1999) argues that the reason certain acts appear as natural within a particular culture is that those acts present themselves as originary. Further, these acts achieve the effect of being natural by the repetition of their performances within a social system dependent on numerous intersecting performances. One might well ask: How is change possible under these circumstances? If what is considered normal becomes so through the repetition of acts, then to disrupt the repetition is to resist normativity. Not repeating, enacting alternative performances, and other mechanisms can serve to disrupt the flow of events that sustain a presumption of the natural. The radical potential of a Jewish queer ritual is the possibility of just such a disruption.

We must note that the radical potential of this disruption does not have to topple a unitary hegemonic idea or practice. In order to be part of deep social change, a particular counter-performance need not succeed in stopping the oppressive performances for all and for all time. The question to be asked is not what performances either change the status quo fully or not. Such an either or notion of revolutionary work too easily leads to despair and reinstates us in the world of impossibilities. On the other hand, it might be more helpful to develop alternative performances that expose the natural for its constructed nature, and/or those that begin to enable further empowering performances. On this point Butler is likely to agree with anarchist reinterpetations of the relationship between what is seen as impossible and that which is possible. Aspirations, resistance, and creative alternatives crumble under the crushing force of the IMPOSSIBLE. But a disruption of the repetition brings the otherwise impossible notion of fundamental change back in relation with the possible. Butler does not write of denaturalization "simply out of a desire to play with language or prescribe theatrical antics in the place of 'real' politics . . . (as if theatre and politics are always distinct). It was done from a desire to live, to make life possible, and to rethink the possible as such" (1999, p. xx).

Repetition plays a significant role in Butler's understanding of normativity and its possible disruption and becomes compelling for those involved in theatre and ritual innovation. One reason performance art has been seen as "not real art" is that a performance "event" cannot be repeated in the same way twice. But who is to say that Karen Findley's wearing a dress made of meat-steaks outside the Miss America Contest transformed consciousness any less than a (re)production of Shakespeare's *The Merry Wives of Windsor*? Repetition is part of what makes ritual–Jewish and other religious rituals in particular–so powerful. Knowing your community has engaged such acts over thousands of years carries great weight for many people. This weight can often contribute to what feels so grounding about long-practiced rituals. Yet, this weight can also be part of what might feel burdensome about certain oppressive aspects of ritual. Depending on the context, any innovation in a ritual might be experienced as radical. But those involved in creative ritual work often struggle with whether or not new rituals (or new aspects of old rituals) are sufficiently radical if they themselves are not repeatable. Some new rituals are developed for one-time purposes. Other developments are intended to supplant traditional rituals altogether. As a radical proposal in ritual theory itself, I do not think the political potential of a ritual innovation rests on whether or not the innovation is repeatable. In the case of a be-coming out ritual, for example, the JQTT discussed many options.

One might envision a be-coming out ritual in a particular community as a one-time performance. One can incorporate a be-coming out ritual during the celebration of the Jewish New Year or new moon, both of which have long symbolized renewal and growth. Situating a be-coming out ritual at these times relies on the power of the traditional Jewish calendar. Some have suggested that such a ritual be scheduled during U.S. Coming Out Day/Week. This option is still situated in a repeatable yearly cycle, but one that ties Jewish needs into the development of secular queer culture. A be-coming out ritual may happen one time in your life or may be introduced into a regular cycle within a community. A community may decide to hold a be-coming out ritual among its repertoire to be conducted as deemed necessary. Some communities might like the ritual repeated the same way each time or they might like to develop new versions. Some individuals might be present performance after performance. In other cases the changing makeup of the community participating might give the ritual its freshness.

Not one of these choices is right or wrong. Butler is careful to warn us that "subversive performances always run the risk of becoming deadening clichés through their repetition and, most importantly, through their repetition within commodity culture where 'subversion' carries market value" (1999, p. xxi). For our purposes, we might say that subversively new rituals cannot be packaged and reperformed without attention to context. Instead, communities ought to be encouraged to ask questions regarding what will make *this* ritual most transformative for them at the time. Relying on anarchist plays on spontaneity and planned programs, like those in the JQTT, others might come to see that the variety of ritual innovations possible can even give traditional blessings, liturgy, and prayer deeper meaning.

MOVING ON

Queer Jews and others are taking ritual seriously as part of queer spiritual life, celebration, and liberation. In this article I have argued that we need to keep our new ideas and practices in the religious realm in mutually empowering relation to new ideas in secular and self-consciously political theory. With the assistance of secular critical theory, let us take a moment to return to the specific idea of reclaiming the mikvah for queer Jews. A group of queer Jews may develop a mikvah ritual for a one-time experience, or repeat it cyclically. In the traditional version, a person going into the mikvah is naked and checked carefully for any hairs or particles that would come between one's body and the water. Women have often found this process humiliating. Queers and all women could use mikvah as a time to reconnect to our bodies and our sexuality, turning what has often become the legalistic "checking" into a celebration.

Jewish queers often express the need to redefine the spaces and textures of what have traditionally been designated as holy and profane. Although some might find this unappealing or too controversial, a group might purposely include wearing or dipping into the water something which would have traditionally suggested impurity. Ritually dripping a drop of lubricant into the water would make the mikvah halachically (in Jewish law) unkosher (unsuitable for ritual use) but participants might see it as a way to enliven the "living waters" with a symbol of queer (and hopefully safe!) sex. For those who have lived in this age of AIDS such a moment of purification which points directly to queer sex could be particularly empowering. As another idea, in the traditional ceremony individuals take three dunks, reciting a blessing and completely submerging oneself in the body of water. As a group ritual a community may reclaim the three submersions. Together they could rewrite the blessing to address three aspects of import to the group. Each submersion could be named, with all invited to dunk for two of the three, and one specifically reserved for those newly coming out in some sphere of their lives. In this way linkages across members in a community and in the processes of be-coming out can be explicitly acknowledged while also attending to the special needs of those "newly" be-coming queer. Experiencing freedom with one's body and sexuality in the context of the ritual can be part of the process of doing so in many aspects of one's life beyond the intentionally ritualized time/space. Facing others in one's community while experiencing one's power enables one to tap into power in life and situations beyond the religiously ritualized moment. Dealing directly with issues of oppression and liberation in the context of a group ritual can foster active engagement with the politics of oppression and liberation in society at large. How else can we utilize ritual innovation in the service of our spiritual needs as well as the process of revolutionary social transformation?

To bring the discussion to a temporary close, I would like to take conscious note of the very Jewish mode of answering questions with questions. For future work, we might ask what repetitions are central to the oppression of queer Jews in particular. What presumptions of "nature" must queer Jews dislodge in order to live more freely as Jewish queers? What kinds of ritual performances can disrupt these repetitions, in different contexts and in different ways? What sorts of performative disruptions can denaturalize that which is natural in the sociocultural context in which queer Jews live, make meaning, participate in community, and therefore constitute an ever contingent and historically specific universe for different queer Jews? Do specific groups, such as lesbians or bisexuals, have different needs than other groups? Do aspects of different lesbian lives challenge Jewish normative rituals in particular ways?

By posing these and other questions and opening a dialogue in terms slightly different from both the GLBTQ normative coming out narrative and uncritical ritual makers, Jewish lesbian and queer ritual innovations can serve as a productive encounter between the spiritual and the secular in many of our lives. If ritual is to be one aspect of making the impossible possible, I am hoping that through engagement with these different sets of questions, that lesbian and queer Jews (as well as any others) may develop concrete rituals that they find spiritually fulfilling and politically revolutionary. I have used the specific example here of coming out rituals discussed over time in the Jewish Queer Think Tank and performed in different ways by various JQTT members. I intend, by assessing the potential political function of ritual itself, that the work of the JQTT might also have wider application. It is my hope that our questions stimulate further questioning for others in their own overlapping communities.

ACKNOWLEDGMENTS

The author would like to thank Eric Cohen and particularly Dawn Rose for their comments on earlier drafts. She is grateful to H. Mark Roelofs, Jan Cohen-Cruz, Augusto Boal, and all those who have taught me about political theatre. She also appreciates the many women, queers, and others with whom I have created and participated in rituals over the years and particularly acknowledge the work of havurot and the National Havurah Institute as well as Jewish feminist groups such as the Jewish Feminist Resource Center at the National Council of Jewish Women, Ma'yan, and B'not Esh for what they have taught (and are continuing to teach) me about ritual innovation. She also wants to thank all of those involved in Ma'yan's Jewish Feminist Research Group, those who attended the special session on this work in progress, and particularly Jennifer Danby and Ruti Kadish for their thoughtful and encouraging reviews.

NOTES

1. Those present at the particular JQTT meetings at which we discussed ritual were, in addition to myself: Eric Cohen, Tamara Cohen, Miryam Kabakov, Gwynn Kessler, Tani Meir, Elliot Pilshaw, David Rogoff, Dawn Robinson Rose, Abigail Ruby, Jonathan Springer, and Laurie Zimmerman.

2. Of course, many of the people who began Jewish feminist ritual innovation were (or are now) also GLTBQ.

3. For Marx's critique of this tact, see his analysis of Critical-Utopian Socialism in the *Communist Manifesto* (1967, pp. 114-118).

4. Dawn Rose's (1998) work on Hanna Levy Haas illustrates this point well. Haas was a communist philosopher who was interned in a concentration camp by the Nazis for being Jewish. With her earlier training in communist theory and strategizing she was able to organize the Jewish women in the camp. See also Haas (1982).

5. For a discussion of these ideas and practices in historical perspective, see Buber (1949).

6. Brecht is famous for breaking down the "wall" between audience and players in an attempt to be more conscious of, and utilize, theatre in radical politics. See, for example, Brecht (1964). Boal's techniques push Brecht's work further in attempting to increasingly democratize theatre and better use drama in political practice.

7. For a critical discussion of revolution and post-modernism in this sense, see Buker (1999, pp. 149-152).

8. As an interesting analysis along these lines, see Mitchell's (1988) critique of the role of World's Fairs in the colonizing process.

9. Schechter's (1985) work on clowning, politics, and theatre is a helpful illustration of Butler's (1999) ideas concerning the transformative political potential of performativity and parody.

10. Although beyond the scope of this article, readers might find interesting that this discussion stimulated a sub-conversation on using the Jewish holiday Purim for such events. At Purim, Jews traditionally put on skits and plays on or inspired by the holiday and its story. We asked, how might we utilize the plays performed at Purim to expose the performances of everyday life that tend to appear natural? The queer potential here is great given the idea that Purim may be seen as a paradigmatic "coming out" narrative (See, for example, Sedgwick, 1994).

REFERENCES

Boal, A. (1985). *Theatre of the oppressed.* New York: Theatre Communications Group.

Boal, A. (2001). *Hamlet and the baker's son: My life in theatre and politics.* New York and London: Routledge.

Brecht, B. (1964). *Brecht on theatre.* New York: Hill and Wang.

Buber, M. (1949). *Paths in utopia.* New York: Macmillan Publishing Company.

Buker, E. A. (1999). *Talking feminist politics: Conversations of law, science and the postmodern.* New York and London: Rowan & Littlefield Publishers, Inc.

Butler, J. (1999). *Gender trouble: Feminism and the subversion of identity* (10th Anniversary Edition). New York and London: Routledge.

Finley, K. (1992). *Shock treatment.* San Francisco: City Lights.

Goldman, E. (1969). *Anarchism and other essays.* New York: Dover Publications, Inc.

Haas, H. L. (1982). *Belsen diary.* Brighton, England: Harvester Press.

Marx, K., & Engels, F. (1967). *The communist manifesto.* New York: Penguin Books.

Mitchell, T. (1988). *Colonising Egypt.* Cambridge and New York: Cambridge University Press.

Phelan, S. (1994). *Getting specific: Postmodern lesbian politics.* Minneapolis and London: University of Minnesota Press.

Rose, D. (1998). "Inmate ethics at Bergen Belsen: The measure of humanity in Hanna Levy-Haas' holocaust philosophy." Paper presented at the 10th Conference of North American and Cuban Philosophers and Social Scientists. Havana, Cuba.

Schechter, J. (1985). *Dubrov's pig: Clowns, politics and theatre.* New York: Theatre Communications Group.

Sedgwick, E. K. (1994). *Epistemology of the closet.* London: Penguin.

The New Religious Rite:
A Symbolic Interactionist Case Study
of Lesbian Commitment Rituals

Krista B. McQueeney

SUMMARY. Despite the legal and religious establishment's denial of rights and recognition to same-gender couples, many lesbians and gay men are adapting and/or creating their own rituals to affirm their commitments to each other. This article uses participant observation of a black lesbian couple's shower and holy union ceremony to explore the multiple and competing meanings attached to the ritualistic symbols and narratives they incorporated. I seek to complicate the existing framework, in which rituals are held to produce feelings of belonging for participants and serve as vehicles for the social transformation of marginalized groups (e.g., Driver, 1991). By adapting and appropriating ritualistic ele-

Krista B. McQueeney is a graduate student in sociology at UNC-Chapel Hill. Her dissertation uses participant observation and in-depth interviewing to examine religious experiences, strategies for reconciling religious and sexual identities, and collective identity negotiation in two LGBT-affirming mainline Protestant congregations in the South.

Address correspondence to: Krista B. McQueeney, Dept. of Sociology, UNC-Chapel Hill, Campus Box 3210, Chapel Hill, NC 27599-3210 (E-mail: kristamcq@msn.com).

Author note: Special thanks to my advisor, Sherryl Kleinman, for her unwavering support and helpful suggestions on my work and to all of the congregation members who allowed me into their church and without whose insights this work would not be possible.

[Haworth co-indexing entry note]: "The New Religious Rite: A Symbolic Interactionist Case Study of Lesbian Commitment Rituals." McQueeney, Krista B. Co-published simultaneously in *Journal of Lesbian Studies* (Harrington Park Press, an imprint of The Haworth Press, Inc.) Vol. 7, No. 2, 2003, pp. 49-70; and: *Lesbian Rites: Symbolic Acts and the Power of Community* (ed: Ramona Faith Oswald) Harrington Park Press, an imprint of The Haworth Press, Inc., 2003, pp. 49-70. Single or multiple copies of this article are available for a fee from The Haworth Document Delivery Service [1-800-HAWORTH, 9:00 a.m. - 5:00 p.m. (EST). E-mail address: docdelivery@haworthpress.com].

49

ments often used in heterosexual weddings, I argue that this couple and their ritual coordinators succeeded in creating a sense of social order, "communitas" (Turner, 1969), and personal and social transformation for some participants. However, I also suggest that the achievement of these functions hinged on the creation of symbolic out-groups and the reproduction of social conventions around gender, the family, and the "appropriate" expression of sex in marriage, which diminished the experience of communitas and social transformation for other participants. Future research should focus on the competing expectations and interpretations participants bring to their experiences of rituals and the ways in which existing structures of power and authority may limit rituals' social functionality, creation of communitas, and revolutionary potential. *[Article copies available for a fee from The Haworth Document Delivery Service: 1-800-HAWORTH. E-mail address: <docdelivery@haworthpress.com> Website: <http://www.HaworthPress.com> © 2003 by The Haworth Press, Inc. All rights reserved.]*

KEYWORDS. Ritual, lesbian, African American, religion, commitment ceremony

Debates over gay and lesbian marriage have raged through courts, legislatures, religious bodies, businesses, and a host of other U.S. establishments in the past decade. In response to this unprecedented dialogue, some employers, insurance companies, and municipalities have begun to offer domestic partner benefits, and the state of Vermont created a legal category of civil union to recognize same-sex couples. In the face of this political advancement, political and mainline religious institutions have been resistant to the notion of formally recognizing same-gender relationships. In 1996, the United States Congress passed and President Clinton signed into law the Defense of Marriage Act, which prohibits federal acknowledgment of same-gender unions and permits states to disregard licenses issued in other states. Thirty-five legislatures have also enacted state level "defense of marriage" laws restricting marriage to heterosexuals only (Ferdinand, 2001). Moreover, none of the historically established, mainline religious denominations in the United States has officially come out in support of gay and lesbian unions (Witham, 2000). Perhaps not surprisingly, increased visibility and acceptance of lesbian and gay people and their families in society at large has given rise to a backlash in political and mainline religious circles (Mohr, 1997). This backlash rests upon the assumption that gay and lesbian relationships are subordinate, if not inherently threatening, to family life based on heterosexual marriage (Oswald, 2000).

Despite these retrenchments, gay and lesbian couples across the nation are planning and performing their own ceremonies to celebrate their love for and commitment to each other, albeit with few or no accompanying legal benefits (Lewin, 1998; Sherman, 1992). As well, many ministers and rabbis have begun to perform "holy union" ceremonies in noncompliance with their denominational policies. Through ethnographic case study this article examines the multiple religious, cultural, and racial identity meanings incorporated in and emanating from one such celebration of commitment–a black[1] lesbian couple's "shower" and holy union ceremony. By analyzing the meanings this couple attempted to evoke in their celebrations of commitment–which occurred within the larger context of a predominantly black, LGBT[2]-affirming, ecumenical Christian church in the South–as well as the meanings ritual narratives and symbols may have held for those who attended the ceremony, I explore several questions. First, why was a holy union ceremony important to this couple, even when they gained no tangible social privileges or legal rights as a result? Second, what rituals and symbols did they choose to incorporate, and how did those who attended experience these ritualistic elements? Third, what do their ritual practices and narratives suggest about the intersections of race, sexuality, and religious ritual? And finally, did the rituals they employed in their holy union challenge, reconstruct, or reproduce social conventions?

METHODOLOGY

The shower and holy union ceremonies analyzed for this paper were drawn from a larger ethnography of a 65-member LGBT-affirming Christian congregation in the South conducted between August 1998 and September 2001. Almost all active congregation members identified as lesbian, gay, bisexual, or transgender. Seventy percent were African American and 30% were white. Over 90% of regular worshippers were female, and their ages ranged from 14 to 71.

Founded in 1997, the church was a self-described ecumenical Christian congregation that embraced one triune God composed of three "persons"–God, the Parent-Creator; Jesus Christ, Son of God; and the Holy Spirit, Sustainer. The central idea in the church's theology was faith, and many of the African American lesbian pastor's sermons and congregation members' testimonies incorporated Biblical and experiential lessons regarding the benefits of a personal relationship with Jesus Christ. Liturgically, the congregation celebrated an open communion every Sunday, frequent baptisms and laying on of hands, and the pastor occasionally presided over holy union ceremonies, which were usually held outside the context of worship services. While members drew from a variety of religious traditions, church practices were distinctive in the recurrent use of charismatic healing, lay testifying and witnessing, a call-and-response style of praise, and the performance of spirituals and civil rights anthems.

The shower and holy union ceremony were observed on two consecutive weekends during July of 2001. Both members of the united couple were active leaders in the congregation, and one was the congregation's pastor. Both had extensive social ties to the local LGBT community. The holy union ceremony was held on the sixth anniversary of the day they met, and they had been in a committed relationship for almost five years at the time of the ceremony. As a congregational ethnographer and friend, I attended the shower by invitation and the holy union through an open invitation that was extended to all worshippers in the congregation. Members of the congregation were aware of my research objectives and I requested their consent to be quoted anonymously when appropriate. Following the holy union ceremony, I spoke with both members of the couple to gain clarification on some aspects of the ceremony, and both read and commented on an earlier draft of this paper.

Following Blumer (1969), I employed a symbolic interactionist perspective in my fieldwork–I immersed myself in participants' social reality and analyzed the processes, communications, and practices in which they engaged. Comprehensive field-notes were collected immediately upon exiting the field and were supplemented and refined by continued questioning of and informal conversation with church members and the lesbian couple for whom the shower and holy union were celebrated.

Approximately 32 pages of field-notes were collected and transcribed based on observation of these events. In coding and analyzing the data, I focused on aspects of the rites that informed the dominant scheme of ritual functionality–order, *communitas*, and transformation. A perspective of intersectionality (Collins, 1998) also informed the analysis. As Collins notes, an interpretive framework that focuses on the intersectionality of unjust power relations seeks to understand how connected systems of oppression shape individuals' experiences and to go beyond race-, class-, or gender-only approaches to social phenomena. To the extent that the "initiated" couple was positioned within intersecting systems of racism, sexism, and heterosexism, I tried to pay particular attention to whether and how they positioned themselves within these intersecting systems of oppression. My findings are not generalizable to any larger population, and are not intended to represent all holy union ceremonies for gay and/or lesbian couples in the United States.

DESCRIPTION OF THE SHOWER AND HOLY UNION CEREMONY

Both the shower and holy union ceremony were held on church grounds because of the religious significance it held for the couple. The shower occurred on a Saturday night in a large, open room in the church's office space and was attended, via invitation, by approximately 25 friends (21 women, both lesbian and heterosexual, and 4 gay men). A congregation member, also a black lesbian, who was a close friend of the couple, organized the shower. She cooked, decorated the room, made opening and closing remarks, organized interactive activities, and decorated a large chest bearing a photograph of the couple and the painted slogan, "Swept away by friends and family," where the gifts were placed.

The mood at the shower was relaxed and casual. It involved no pretense of secrecy–both members of the couple were aware of when and where the shower would take place, had input into the activities and the menu, and had established gift registries. They entered together at the time the shower was scheduled to begin and mixed and mingled until all the guests arrived, at which time the hostess welcomed everyone with an opening speech. She congratulated the couple and voiced her support for their upcoming holy union. A buffet supper was then served, before which the partner who was the congregation's pastor said a blessing. Guests ate at two large tables set up in a narrow "V" formation in the center of the room so that they could interact with those across from and beside them. No alcohol was served by request of the couple.

After supper, the hostess directed everyone to the left of the room, where chairs and couches were organized for seating. First, the hostess explained the "jumping the broom" ritual to make certain that everyone understood its meaning and historical roots. Then guests lined up to add their own decoration to the broom using the white ribbons, flowers, and small plastic doves provided. Next the hostess led guests in a series of break-the-ice types of interactive games. After approximately an hour, the hostess directed everyone into the area to the far right of the room where the gifts were stacked (inside the chest and overflowing onto the floor) and both partners opened their gifts. They made it clear that they had separate gift requests–one partner for the household supplies and the other for gadgets such as an indoor grill and DVD player. As they opened their gifts and collected them in their separate heaps, the hostess made a list of the gifts while another guest attached the ribbons and bows onto a paper plate for a mock bouquet one partner was to carry during the ceremony rehearsal. Finally, the pastor thanked everyone for coming and for showing support and love for her and her partner. The shower lasted slightly over two hours.

The holy union ceremony was held on the following Saturday afternoon in a large sanctuary adjacent to where worship services were usually held. The couple and their holy union party (attendants, soloists, ushers) had attended a rehearsal dinner the previous evening as is customary in many heterosexual weddings. Approximately 150 friends, co-workers, and church members attended the ceremony and reception. Written invitations had been sent, and announcements had been made at church during the weeks preceding the holy union inviting all worshippers to attend. Immediately outside the door of the sanctuary in the church foyer stood an easel on which photographs of both brides' deceased parents were displayed. "Songs from the Heart" played as guests entered; two ushers in white dresses escorted guests to their seats. Six attendants–five women and one man, all close friends of the couple–participated in the ceremony wearing black tuxedos. There was an enclosed room in the rear of the sanctuary for latecomers–the couple was determined that the ceremony would begin on time and did not allow latecomers to enter the church–and this room became quite full after the service began. A white lesbian UFMCC minister, also a close friend of the couple's, officiated. The ceremony was relatively reserved in tone and included several religious symbols and rituals. It began with the officiate lighting a candle to the tune of "Love Never Dies." Then came the entrance of two attendants in succession, each of whom proceeded down the aisle and onto the altar to light a candle, first in remembrance of one partner's deceased parents and the next in remembrance of the other's deceased father. The remaining four attendants then proceeded down the side aisles, and next entered the couple, arm in arm down the center aisle to the song "Beautiful Girl." Both wore champagne-colored dresses and carried small bouquets of flowers (one a traditional cream-colored rose bouquet and the other a small bouquet of two hot pink and yellow flowers, tied with multicolored ribbons). After welcoming the guests, the officiate read two Scriptures–1 Corinthians 13 and Song of Songs 4–both of which emphasized the supremacy and spiritual transcendence of love. Next the couple exchanged personal vows each had written, and then they exchanged rings. Before serving communion to the partners, who knelt at a small white wooden altar constructed for the ceremony, the minister made a "charge to the congregation" requesting a congregational vow of support for the couple. Finally the minister pronounced them united in holy union, saying "I present to you [the couple], life partners" and they kissed. At various junctures in the ceremony, several guests, as well as both partners and the minister, began to cry. In all, the ceremony lasted about 50 minutes.

Following the ceremony, guests moved outside to the patio separating the two church sanctuaries for a champagne toast. In the center of the patio area was a small table, where a tall circular wire frame covered with white translucent material resembling a bride's veil stood. Inside the frame were several butterflies–participants were invited to raise the veil to release a butterfly and say a prayer to bless the couple's new life together. Caviar and other hors d'oeuvres were served and glasses of champagne handed out by two male "waiters" and a female "champagne attendant," all of whom were dressed in tuxedos. Although the sky was gray and it was drizzling slightly, all of the attendants, ushers, and soloists made toasts as guests stood outside, congratulating and wishing the couple spiritual blessings. A few referred to the rain with toasts like "to the wet and the dry" and "rain is a blessing because it washes away all the bad and makes room for the sun." After about 15 minutes of toasts, everyone filtered inside to the smaller sanctuary, where a buffet dinner was laid out on a long table to the far right of the sanctuary. The "head table" where the brides and attendants sat–and in back of which a multitiered white wedding cake was placed–ran horizontally along the altar space at the back of the sanctuary. About 20 long tables were arranged pointing vertically toward the head table for open seating among guests during dinner. After dinner, tables were pushed back to clear a space in front of the altar for dancing.

ANALYSIS

The Creation of Order

Rites of passage, according to van Gennep (1960), lessen the social disorganization inherent to the liminal, or in-between, phase of status or position changes. Apprehension and a lack of structure characterize the liminal phase, and rituals reduce the sense of chaos by reestablishing order and dividing time into discrete and recognizable periods (Leach, 1966). Rites of lesbian commitment-like other rites of passage–can organize the progression of same-sex relationships and reduce the anxiety that may inhere in the act of committing oneself to a life partnership. Here, I will discuss two aspects of order created by the observed rituals–what Rappaport (1979) calls "symbolic" and "factitive" order.

Symbolic order. According to Rappaport (1979), rituals create a sense that the world is structured by explicitly marking transitions of time and space. Rites of commitment may mark the seasons of lesbian relationships and life stages more explicitly than private vows or markers of commitment such as moving in with a partner. They are formal acts in which two people intentionally pledge their devotion and love for one another in front of a community of supporters and, in religious ceremonies, in front of God. The social nature of commitment rituals presents an opportunity for lesbian couples to find validation and support from their families of origin and friends (Lewin, 1998), as well as to express and unite around group identities linked to race, religion, sexuality, family tradition, and/or other sources (Oswald, 2001). The clarity of the couple's intentions, the formality of the occasion, the ritual's expressive character, and the public forum in which it occurs all signify the commitment as an important life transition and a vehicle to a higher state of being.

Two sub-rituals within the commitment ceremony also contributed to a sense of order. The first was the memorializing of deceased parents through the display of photographs and performance of candle lighting. This not only evoked a sense of order in their family tradition and heritage, but also a sense of stability in and connection to their racial identities. No living family of origin members attended the shower or holy union ceremony, and one partner spoke openly about her family's continuing disapproval of their lesbian relationship. Said one partner when I asked why they paid homage to their deceased parents:

> If they had been alive they would have been with us physically, but they were with us in spirit instead and we wanted to honor that.

By paying homage only to their deceased parents, they may have attempted not only to convey their continuing attachment to and respect for their families of origin, but also to create the image that their families were actually supportive of their decision to join in holy union. Had they paid symbolic respect to the partner's mother who was still living or to their siblings (all of whom chose not to attend), it may have stimulated questions about family members' absence from the union and the lack of approval and support their absence implied.

While many parents of gay and lesbian couples do not attend holy union ceremonies (Lewin, 1998), the act of showing respect to their families of origin, even when they were not present and may not have supported their union, may be an especially critical imperative for lesbians of color. The values of paying respect to one's elders, family, and heritage have particularly strong roots in black churches (Brown, 2000) and the display of photographs definitively linked the couple to and declared pride in their family and racial heritage. Furthermore, it constructed the couple as respectful, aware and appreciative of their roots, and as supportive of–and supported by–their families. Through this symbolic act, the couple attempted to challenge the stigma that gay and lesbian relationships threaten the nuclear family and that black lesbians have "sold out" to white society or "forgotten where they came from" due to their homosexuality (Icard, 1985, p. 86). Their symbolic displays of respect to deceased family members also created a sense of order by anchoring them in the social continuity of their nuclear families (Kahn & Antonucci, 1981).

The similarity of these rites to conventional heterosexual weddings and bridal showers also contributed to the creation of social order. One of the partners recounted all the measures they had taken so that their shower and holy union would be free of "heterosexual content"–their choice of dresses, the decision to include both partners in the shower, their opposition to having a traditional "bachelorette party," and their rejection of various gifts recommended for the holy union party which they deemed too heterosexual. Despite the couple's attempts to send the message that "you don't have to look heterosexual in order for the ceremony to be real," as one partner asserted, the irony was that they co-opted symbols and meanings that were deeply entrenched in heterosexual weddings and bridal showers. Their desire to evoke a sense of these events as being "traditional," "special," and "spiritual" may have limited how inventive and nonconformist they felt they could be while still adhering to convention and eliciting a positive response from the various guests who attended.

In both the shower and the holy union, the couple appropriated and/or adapted several elements from traditionally heterosexual rites of commitment. Why would they do this, given their resistance to traditionally heterosexual symbols? As a rule, rituals must provide some vestige of familiarity and reflect shared values so as not to be perceived as "hollow" (Roberts, 1988). According to Roberts, a ritual can be considered "hollow" when the symbols constructed are not congruent with the symbols desired. Commitment ceremonies are new and sometimes unique adaptations of traditional rites of commitment, but the ritual coordinators' and participants' notions of the "symbols desired" were still shaped by their previous experiences with other ritualistic celebrations, for example weddings, bridal showers, and the conventional phases of commitment more generally. The couple and their ritual coordinators were cognizant of this in planning the ceremony, and they attempted to incorporate ritualistic elements that guests would recognize as exalting love and showing their respectfulness and dignity, while simultaneously acknowledging their lesbianism.

With few exceptions, the rituals they incorporated were co-opted and/or adapted from African American and modern heterosexual weddings–jumping the broom, the Native American custom of releasing the butterflies to signify liberation in their new life together, the multitiered white wedding cake, the exchange of rings, the attendants dressed in tuxedos symbolically "giving away" the brides (adaptive of the father's traditional role), and a host of more subtle ritualistic elements in both the shower and holy union ceremony. In addition, although they used various displays (e.g., both wearing dresses) to make it clear that they identified as a female-female couple, one aspect of the vow may have struck some participants as reminiscent of the bride's vow of "obedience" to the groom. One partner (the office manager) said to the other (the pastor), "I promise to cherish, respect, protect, nurture, honor, and be your love slave forever." This statement was intended to be comical, but its ambiguity left it up to individual interpretation as to whether it was reminiscent of the bride's vow of obedience, sought to poke fun at the bride's submissive duty, or bore no relation to it and was purely in jest.

The couple also incorporated various elements illustrative of the consumerism that pervades heterosexual weddings such as the photographer, the videographer, gift registries, diamond wedding bands, and caviar and other gourmet hors d'oeuvres. Just as many heterosexual couples consult bridal planners for various items that will give their weddings a personal touch (Currie, 1993), this couple attempted to personalize their ceremony by researching rituals, dresses, tuxedos for the attendants, color schemes, decorations, and other accoutrements that would make the ceremony unique and reflective of their values and identities. One outcome of this planning was that, although the ceremony was relatively modest and certainly drew attention to the religious nature of their commitment, aspects of the consumerist wedding culture were integrated that made costs higher than the couple had anticipated. The couple included these elements to signify their celebrations as special and to evoke a sense of the familiar and traditional, all of which contributed to the sense of symbolic order they hoped to achieve through these ritualistic enactments.

As well, the couple's desire for a sense of the "familiar" guided their ritual enactment. The sequence in which rituals are performed is essential to their function of creating order (Driver, 1991; van Gennep, 1960). Their progress from pre-commitment, commitment, and post-commitment rites was intended to evoke a sense of familiarity, adherence to convention, and to order time into discrete periods. Friends organized a shower to celebrate their upcoming union, the couple held a rehearsal dinner for the holy union party the evening before the ceremony, and they took a short and unpretentious honeymoon afterwards. Although it is less common for lesbians to conceptually order their commitments according to what might be considered traditionally heterosexual cycles, there is a sense of order and timing inherent in these enactments that places the more ambiguous stages of lesbian commitment within an established moral structure.

The enactment of the holy union ceremony itself also contributed to and reflected the sense of order the couple tried to evoke in committing to each other. As one member of the couple told me, "You know when you're a little girl, you just have these dreams and you plan what your wedding's going to be like . . . I wasn't going to let my sexuality get in the way of having everything I wanted." Her statement suggests that she viewed the holy union as a form of resistance to heterosexism–she was entitled to a wedding (of sorts) and she wasn't going to allow the law, social prejudice, or anything else to prevent her from having it. At the same time, her comment implies a striving for order and validation that recalls traditional feminine socialization. She grew up "dreaming about what [her] wedding [was] going to be like," and experiencing a holy union ceremony enabled her to claim a sense of order in and absolute commitment to her relationship, as well as a sense of fulfilling traditional expectations as a woman. Her comments calls to mind the lesbian mothers that Lewin (1994) interviewed, who simultaneously resisted gendered constructions of sexuality by challenging the equation of homosexuality with unnaturalness and reproduced them by complying with conventional feminine expectations of motherhood.

Moreover, the couple's friends held a shower before the holy union, similar to a heterosexual bridal shower, which again marked a key point in the liminal phase–their embrace into a supportive community of LGBT friends and family. It should be noted that most shower guests were long-term couples. While Cheal (1988) characterizes the female heterosexual bridal shower as a rite of passage into the adult female community, the shower for this couple might be better characterized as initiating the couple into a community of committed same-sex couples. Rather than marking a transition into adulthood, this shower seemed to signify the couple's entrance into a mutually supportive community of lesbian and gay partners, some having been consecrated by holy union and others not yet having done so, but all seemingly bound by that expectation.

Factitive order. In addition to symbolizing order, ritual creates the scaffolding that enables organization to appear (Driver, 1991). This constitutive aspect of ritual is what Rappaport (1979) called factitive order, and I observed it in several aspects of the commitment ceremony. First of all, congregational support and solidarity promoted the emotional, psychological, and spiritual wellbeing both of the couple and their guests. Because the couple's families of origin were not present at or supportive of their union, their chosen LGBT family, particularly in the church, provided the nurturance and validation of their relationship that their families of origin were unable or unwilling to provide. Because black churches have provided significant refuge from societal racism (Comstock, 2001) the fact that this family was both supportive and spiritual may have been particularly important to the couple themselves and to many members of their chosen family.

Another element of factitive order was gift exchange. Although they had already lived together for over two years before these events, the use of gift registries provided material support for their relationship that had been previously unavailable. In addition to promoting solidarity between the couple and their shower and holy union guests (see Cheal, 1988), the provision of gifts reproduced the material benefits of marriage, and the contemporary capitalist notion of "family" as a unit isolated from communal living. It also firmly embedded this ceremony within the astoundingly prosperous wedding industry, which was estimated to bring in profits between $30 to $50 billion dollars in 2000 (Dixon, 2000).

In addition to materializing their relationship and promoting solidarity within their specific community, the shower and holy union ceremony contributed to the dominant social order by reproducing conventions around monogamy and couplehood. Certainly, these celebrations challenged the exclusivity of heterosexual marriage and made claim to a vision of commitment, love, and marriage that included same-gender couples. However, moral and legal regulations defining marriage as the exclusive domain of two mutually committed persons and the exaltation of couplehood were clearly not in question. Such rituals therefore perpetuate the notion that monogamous couplehood is the morally superior way to live and form intimate attachments–the familiar jibes often heard at heterosexual weddings about "who would be next" were abundant. In fact, both of the partners passed on their bouquets–one by throwing it into an expectant crowd of lesbians and the other by making an official presentation to an attendant she called her "white husband." In this way, the ritualistic celebrations of holy union and commitment reestablished monogamy and couplehood as relational ideals that all couples, heterosexual and non-heterosexual, should strive for and exalt.

PERSONAL AND SOCIAL TRANSFORMATION

Ritual has the potential not only to bring about personal transformations into a new–and generally higher–state or position, but also to engender social change through ritual processes of transformation (Baumann, 1992; Driver, 1991). By creating an alternate world in which lesbian commitments are supported, ascribed dignity and value, and recognized as important life cycle transitions, the commitment rituals described here did bring about feelings of personal transformation. One member of the couple asked me:

> Do you see any change in me since the holy union? . . . A few people have said that I seem more at peace and happy with my life and settled in our life together. I even unpacked these boxes I've had in the closet the whole time [my partner] and I have been living together. I just really feel so much more at peace and settled here and just in our life together.

Her comments indicate that the holy union rituals brought her into a state of stability and contentment. Thus, these ritualistic ceremonies facilitated personal growth and conversion into a new, deeper, more assured level of commitment and connection.

While scholars have articulated ritual's potential to bring about social liberation, especially for marginalized groups (e.g., Driver, 1991; Turner, 1986;

Wink, 1986), little empirical research has been conducted to investigate the conditions under which such transformations might be possible. I acknowledge that ritualistic celebrations of lesbian commitment may serve to increase social acceptance of non-heterosexual relationships and possibly even lead to the eventual legalization of same-gender unions or marriage. However, my observations suggest that scholars have not paid adequate attention to how existing social norms and sources of authority may shape, and in fact limit, ritual's potential for social transformation.

One problem is that definitions of adequate social transformation may vary. Some participants in these ritualistic ceremonies surely defined this celebration of lesbian holy union as a social transformation–it involved a broadening of social definitions regarding who is fit to marry and may actually lead to the elimination, or at least the reduction, of stigma on gay and lesbian people and the social and moral value of their relationships. However, I would argue that this is a relatively limited vision of social transformation. As we have seen, this lesbian couple and their supporters did not question the authority of monogamy, the "private and consuming" family, or the moral supremacy of couplehood. In fact, they appealed to and reinforced these sources of existing authority in order to legitimate their union. Perhaps because these were formal, community-wide events in which guests' expectations were presumably shaped by their previous experiences with weddings and bridal showers–and because the couple depended upon dominant ideologies for their own sense of themselves as decent people–their ability to challenge generally accepted norms around monogamy, couplehood, and the isolated nuclear family was thwarted. In their pursuit of order and legitimacy, the lesbian couple and their supporters reinforced and reproduced some of the same oppressive dynamics that contributed to their own oppression, which I would argue constrained their rituals' potential to achieve more fundamental social transformation.

THE QUESTION OF COMMUNITAS

Few scholars have questioned Turner's notion of *communitas*, which posits that ritual actors experience themselves as part of an "undifferentiated, homogeneous whole" (1969, p. 177; but see Baumann, 1992; Oswald, 2001). In this section, I examine the limits of *communitas* by showing how commitment rituals both heightened and diminished a sense of undifferentiated belonging through the marking of symbolic boundaries.

A central dynamic of collective identity formation is the drawing of symbolic boundaries that differentiate in-groups from out-groups (Baumann, 1992; Smith, 1998; Taylor & Whittier, 1992). There were two ritualistic elements of the commitment celebrations in which symbolic boundaries were drawn and feelings of *communitas* produced for some and possibly weakened for others. The first was the traditional African American custom of "jumping the broom," which was included both in the shower (when the broom was decorated) and in the ceremony reception (when the broom was jumped). The custom of jumping the broom was popularized by the televised version of Alex Haley's *Roots*, which depicted rites of self-marrying that slaves initiated in the face of legal prohibitions against slave marriage (Pleck, 2000). In the wake of increased public consciousness, some African Americans began to incorporate the custom in their weddings. Pleck characterizes this custom as a sign of racial consciousness emerging from the Black Nationalist movement and as an implicit statement that black Americans could adopt traditions from slavery instead of searching their "ancestral" African origins for traditions (Pleck, 2000, p. 230). For this lesbian couple, jumping the broom served as both an assertion of their racial identities and an allusion to the subversive nature of their own self-marrying rite. It also heightened bonds of *communitas* for the couple's supporters by drawing symbolic boundaries between themselves and those who denied their ancestors and themselves the right to marry.

At the shower, the hostess made a point of explaining the custom for those who were unaware of its meaning. She said:

> [Jumping the broom] goes back to the times of slavery, when slaves weren't allowed to marry. Later it was used for other illegal marriages, like for mixed-race couples [looks over at a mixed-race lesbian couple]. During slavery, just like it is for us today, the whole community celebrated a wedding. Both the men and the women would make quilts for the bride and the groom, and the women would decorate a broom the night before the wedding. They would put the broom on the front door of the house, and that would be the sign that a wedding was being planned there. Then on the wedding day, the couple would jump over the broom to start their new life together and to sweep away all the ghosts of their past. The wedding was a time of joy and celebration in the community, so we're going to celebrate that with [the couple] right now—what we're going to do next is everyone's going to tie your own ribbon on the broom. . . . That way we can give them our blessings and welcome them to the family as they start this new phase of their lives together.

By explaining the ritual, the hostess attempted to make all present feel involved in its meaning and significance. She also tried to construct all participants as a family whose support was crucial to the couple's sustenance amidst systems of oppression. Further, by identifying the slave self-marrying rituals as a historical precedent to lesbian holy unions, she attempted to impose a sense of order and liberation on the ritualistic celebrations. By evoking symbolic boundaries between blacks and whites and then implicitly between LGBT people and heterosexuals–but then defining these distinctions as less important than family unity–the hostess attempted to heighten bonds of *communitas* among participants in the shower.

Probably, the performance of this custom and the explanation she gave for its connection to the present occasion did heighten most participants' experience of *communitas* by stressing the vital role of community in supporting the lesbian couple in this rite of self-affirmation. All participants were made mutually aware of the subversive nature of the custom and, correspondingly, of lesbian commitment rites. This constructed participants in the shower as the in-group. By emphasizing the antagonism and bigotry of other groups, bonds of mutuality and belonging were amplified among participants. To the extent that the ritual defined whites and heterosexuals as outsiders–i.e., those who denied blacks and/or lesbians the right to marry–it is possible that these ritually constructed boundaries caused some participants in the ritual to feel disconnected from the group. However, it seemed that the hostess' explanation of the custom and her emphasis on the crucial role of community support contributed to feelings of belonging and equality. One shower participant's comments reflected this feeling:

> To be honest, I didn't know what to expect because usually wedding showers are just so phony and I don't want to have anything to do with them. This was the first time I really felt like we were all there to celebrate what's important–their love for each other and God, and our support for them–not just the material gifts or whatever. We have to come together at times like this to support each other's love because we don't get that from too many other people in our lives.

Thus, the broom ritual contributed to participants' feelings of solidarity and *communitas* in part by creating symbolic boundaries between themselves and those who discriminated against LGBT people and/or people of color.

At the beginning of the holy union reception when the couple actually jumped the broom, an attendant explained the ritual in much less detail. She said, "I present to you the happy couple . . . and as in old African traditions, they will now come and jump the broom." Here, the custom was still defined as an expression of racial identity, but its subversive nature was omitted. This may have been intentional, so as not to make whites and/or heterosexual guests feel excluded, or it could have been simply in the interests of brevity. In any event, the lack of explanation caused some guests to feel left out of the ritual enactment. Several guests surrounding me turned to one another with quizzical expressions or to ask each other what the ritual was all about, though I did not overhear or participate in any sustained discussion of the ritual. Those white and/or heterosexual guests who were aware of its significance may also have felt like ritual outsiders, even when they may have respected its performance as an expression of racial identity. I would argue that the ritual succeeded in creating feelings of solidarity, belonging, and communitas for LGBT and/or black guests, particularly those who had been invited to the shower, because they were defined as ritual "insiders." However, its effect was probably not equally constitutive of *communitas* for all guests, and may have actually made those defined as ritual outsiders feel disconnected and left out. My intention here is certainly not to suggest that such expressions of racial and sexual identity are discriminatory or inappropriate, but rather to suggest that they may not have evoked feelings of belonging and solidarity for everyone who participated.

The second set of ritual elements that sought to create *communitas* by drawing symbolic boundaries revolved around traditional constructions of morality. Both celebrations incorporated multiple references to God, Christian morals, and exaltation of Biblical texts as a means of expressing the couple's spiritual identities. By integrating religious symbols, texts, and moral guidelines, the couple and their ritual coordinators sought to construct these occasions as sacred events and to show that they were respectful, honorable people. These ritualistic elements indicated that they were not out to challenge traditional Christian morality, but rather to celebrate a loving, committed, moral relationship that glorified God. I will discuss two ritualistic elements through which the couple attempted to establish themselves as moral while simultaneously defining others as immoral.

One way the couple created symbolic boundaries between themselves and those who were less worthy was by excluding what they defined as the profane from their celebrations, except at times when its inclusion was appropriate according to a traditional Christian framework. By exalting elements of the sacred–such as romantic notions of true love and religious references–and defining elements of the profane–such as sex and alcohol–as off-limits, they attempted to show their adherence to moral order and to define their union as sacred. I will argue that the incorporation of rituals demanding adherence to Christianity and traditional Christian morals drew symbolic boundaries between the ritual in-group of righteous Christians and those who deviated from these ritually constructed norms.

The couple insisted that no alcohol or sexual content be incorporated in the shower. The shower hostess explained to me that at first she had been envisioning the shower as more of a bachelorette party where strippers and alcohol would be involved. When she discovered that both partners would be attending, she had planned interactive activities she thought would be fun but that would still involve sexual content such as giving the couple sexual advice or games that would require some physical contact among guests. However, the couple objected to her plans because they wanted the shower to be respectful and devoid of sexual content, which they associated with heterosexual bachelor and bachelorette parties. Perhaps because the shower occurred during what van Gennep (1960) and Turner (1969) call the liminal phase–the phase of ambiguity before God's blessing had made their union official and authentic–the couple felt that references to sex and the inclusion of alcohol would be inappropriate. When I asked about her reaction to this, one guest at the shower responded:

> Well, I actually agree because when a lot of people think about gays and lesbians, they think promiscuous. We're about love, and we just want our love and commitment to be recognized. We know that God recognizes it, but we have to be careful about what messages we send to other people. We don't want to reinforce anybody's ideas about us–we love and hurt and have sex just like the rest of the world, but we have to let people know that we do it in a way that glorifies God.

Her comments suggest that the exclusion of sex and alcohol was a kind of ritualistic performance through which the group attempted to repudiate stigma. By associating sex and alcohol with heterosexuality, and then defining them as profane and off-limits, the couple attempted to signify the shower and holy union as sacred celebrations of spiritually transcendent love.

On one hand, these ritualistic separations of the sacred from the profane sought to challenge stigmas against gay and lesbian people as hypersexual and threatening to traditional morality. On the other hand, they created symbolic boundaries that distanced ritual participants from those who engaged in drinking or premarital sex. Through the exclusion of these so-called profane elements, the couple intended to signify their shower (and later the holy union ceremony) as different from–and in turn more respectful and authentic than–analogous heterosexual rites such as bachelor and bachelorette parties. However, it might be also said that the couple distanced themselves from supposedly deviant LGBT people who rejected traditional morals around sex and/or drinking. To the extent that these rituals reinscribed symbolic boundaries concerning what kinds of people–heterosexual and non-heterosexual–are to be considered virtuous and allowed full membership, their potential to create a truly inclusive *communitas* was undermined.

Another way the couple sought to show that sacredness characterized their relationship and to reinforce traditional Christian morality as the path to sacredness was through their veneration of Biblical texts in the holy union ceremony. The couple chose two readings: Song of Songs 4 and 1 Corinthians 13, both of which emphasized the spiritual transcendence of love and the "appropriate" expression of sex in marriage. Because of space limitations, I will focus on Song of Songs 4 as an allegory of the lesbian relationship being celebrated and sanctified by God's blessing.

Song of Songs features a dialogue between a simple Jewish woman and her lover, King Solomon. It is a highly intimate expression of their feelings for each other and longing to be together, a dialogue that places sex in its "proper, God-given perspective" (Life Application Study Bible, 1991, p. 1152). It paints their love as ecstatic–Solomon focuses on his lover's beauty and purity and his strong feelings of admiration for her. Using eloquent imagery Solomon tells her:

> You have stolen my heart, my sister, my bride/you have stolen my heart/ with one glance of your eyes,/with one jewel of your necklace. (4:9)

Solomon then goes on to say

> How delightful is your love, my sister, my bride!/How much more pleasing is your love than wine,/and the fragrance of your perfume than any spice! (4:10)

In verse 4:12, Solomon describes his beloved as "a garden locked up," praising her virginity and putting sex in the "appropriate" context of love and marriage (Life Application Study Bible, 1991, p. 1159). Finally, he compares her to a:

> Garden fountain,/a well of flowing water/streaming down from Lebanon. (4:15)

She makes him feel as no earthly pleasure–i.e., wine or fragrant spices–can and is as refreshing to him as a fountain in her purity. Taken together, these verses emphasize Solomon's overwhelming feelings for his beloved and the experience of rebirth she provides him in her purity and sexual innocence. Moreover, this dialogue between the lovers occurs within a broader context of class boundaries between the lovers that cause the bride to feel insecure about her dark skin, which has been interpreted to mean that she probably worked outside in the vineyards (Life Application Study Bible, 1991, p. 1154). But their tremendous love for each other and God's blessing enables the lovers to over-

come social barriers and personal adversity to attain what many have interpreted as an ideal Christian union embodying the purity and sacredness of
love.

The couple chose this passage because it epitomized their own love and
commitment to each other in the face of wider social constraints–constraints
the Biblical narrative exposes as socially constructed and unjust. By placing
their love in a liberatory and religiously sanctioned context–one that involved
sex only within the context of marriage–they attempted to show their adherence to traditional Christian morals and to reestablish those morals as the path
to liberation and sacredness. Just as the power of King Solomon and his un-
named bride's love-with God's help-enabled them to conquer the falsely im-
posed class boundaries that separated them, so too could the rite of holy union
before God sustain the lesbian couple's love for a lifetime in the face of the unjust restrictions placed upon same-gender love. By showing that they adhered
to biblical proscriptions against sex before marriage, the couple defined their
path as a sacred duty–one that, if followed, would guarantee the eternalness of
lesbian unions and God's protection from worldly injustice.

Through what Driver (1991) calls the "ritual mode of performance," the
couple stressed the power of true love to overcome social barriers and directed
attention to the sacredness and transcendence of their love. At the same time,
they and their ritual coordinators defined the path of traditional sexual morality and Christian faith in God as the true vehicle to liberation and sacred connection. By establishing themselves as righteous, traditional Christians who
adhered to Christian prohibitions against premarital sex, the couple created
symbolic boundaries between themselves and the less worthy, which may
have weakened the experience of *communitas* for those in attendance who did
not adhere to traditional Christian morality.

CONCLUSION

In a society that exalts couplehood, marriage, and weddings, it should come
as no surprise that some LGBT people–like the overwhelming majority of heterosexuals–seek to honor and validate their relationships through rites of commitment. Although same-gender commitment ceremonies in the South entail
no conferral of legal rights or wider social recognition, they nevertheless hold
significant symbolic value for some gay and lesbian couples in structuring
their relationships and lives, providing an opportunity to celebrate their relationships with family and friends, and in being recognized as morally worthy
people who make bona fide life commitments to the person they love. In addition, rites of commitment are perceived by many LGBT people as acts of

agency that promise transformation, as something that can be "done" to challenge oppressive institutions and to attain a higher level of commitment and spiritual connection in their relationships. To the extent that Americans pay tribute to and are on many levels judged by their ability to exhibit the individualist attributes of autonomy, self-reliance, and self-improvement (Bellah, 1985), commitment rites offer some gay and lesbian couples the opportunity to determine the course of their own relationships, to achieve a higher status, to choose how and with whom to create families, and to decide how to articulate their identities. Commitment ceremonies may indeed represent an important step on the journey to finding and expressing one's "true self."

Despite the promise lesbian commitment rituals hold for facilitating personal growth, affirmation, and even transformation, I believe it is important to consider their limitations. Because lesbian commitment rituals depend in large part on established rituals and existing sources of social authority for recognition and legitimacy, their potential for transforming existing structures of inequality and creating truly inclusive, equal bonds of *communitas* is constrained by existing norms, ritualistic visions, and the culturally and religiously pluralistic world we inhabit. At the risk of sounding cynical, I would venture to say that perhaps Turner's vision of *communitas* is not an attainable goal or even one we should strive for in the contemporary United States. Surely, as humans we all share a common search for meaning and a sense of belonging. But rituals, by their very nature, exalt some values–to the exclusion–of others and may be incapable of meeting every participant's expectations for belonging.

Despite these limitations of ritual, we should recognize the importance of creating vehicles to consecrate lesbian life. The fact that a mutually supportive, spiritual community of LGBT people of color even exists at all in the South holds promise for the continued molding of visions and questioning of dominant norms and worldviews. Such locales of sustained interaction among people with multiple and competing viewpoints hold promise for social change that grapples with the tensions between sameness and difference. Whether these communities will transform the world is yet to be seen, but their ritual practices, in this author's view, are a step in the right direction.

NOTES

1. One member of the couple has expressed her preference for the term "black" over "African American" because in her view "African American" suggests that black people are not fully American. Accordingly, I use "black" as a descriptive term in this paper.
2. "LGBT" is the term church members use to describe lesbian, gay, bisexual, and transgender people and is therefore the term I employ in this paper. Clearly, identity la-

beling, as with race, is controversial and problematic, particularly because some of the transgender members of the church identify as heterosexual. My intention is not to suggest that there is some inherent similarity among all LGBT people or all people of various races. Rather, when exploring the relationship of LGBT people to social conventions and institutions such as marriage–and the legal and social rights and privileges therein–it is meaningful to distinguish between heterosexuals and non-heterosexuals (see also Oswald, 2000).

REFERENCES

Baumann, G. (1992). Ritual implicates others: Rereading Durkheim in a plural society. In D. DeCoppett (Ed.), *Understanding rituals*. New York: Routledge.

Bellah, R. (1985). *Habits of the heart: Individualism and commitment in American life*. Berkeley, CA: University of California Press.

Blumer, H. (1969). *Symbolic interactionism: Perspective and method*. Berkeley: University of California Press.

Brown, T. F. (2000). *God don't like ugly: African American women handing on spiritual values*. Nashville: Abington Press.

Cheal, D. (1988). Relationships in time: Ritual social structure and the life course. *Studies in Symbolic Interaction, 9*, 83-109.

Collins, P. H. (1998). *Fighting words: African American women and the search for justice*. Minneapolis, MN: University of Minnesota Press.

Comstock, D. (2001). *A whosoever church: Welcoming lesbians and gay men into African American congregations*. London: Westminster John Knox Press.

Currie, D. (1993). Here comes the bride: The making of a 'modern traditional' wedding in western culture. *Journal of Comparative Family Studies, 24*, 403-421.

Dixon, M. (2000, February 8). Wedding industry enjoys millennium boom. [Electronic Version] Found at *http://www.professionaljeweler.com/archives/news/2000/020800story.html* (from Reuters).

Driver, T. (1991). *Magic of ritual: Our need for liberating rites that transform our lives and our communities*. San Francisco, CA: Harper Collins.

Ferdinand, P. (2001, September 4). With Vermont in the lead, controversy progresses: Battle over same-sex unions moves to other states. *Washington Post*, p. A03.

Icard, L. (1985). Black gay men and conflicting social identities: Sexual orientation versus racial identity. *Journal of Social Work and Human Sexuality, 4*, 83-93.

Kahn, R., & Antonucci, T. (1981). Convoys of social support. In Kiesler, J. Morgan, & V. Oppenheimer (Eds.), *Aging and social change*. Orlando, FL: Academic Press.

Leach, E. (1966). Ritualization in man in relation to conceptual and social development. *The philosophical transactions of the Royal Society of London, 29th series, 251*, 403-408.

Lewin, E. (1994). Negotiating lesbian motherhood: The dialectics of resistance and accommodation. In E. Nakano-Glenn, G. Chang, & L. Forcey (Eds.), *Mothering: Ideology, experience, and agency*. New York: Routledge.

Lewin, E. (1998). *Recognizing ourselves: Ceremonies of lesbian and gay commitment*. New York: Columbia University Press.

Life application study Bible. (1991). New International Version. Wheaton, IL: Tyndale Publishers.

Mohr, R. (1997). A gay and straight agenda. In J. Corvino (Ed.), *Same sex: Debating the ethics, science, and culture of homosexuality.* New York: Rowan & Littlefield.

Oswald, R. F. (2000). A member of the wedding? Heterosexism and family ritual. *Journal of Social and Personal Relationships 17*(3), 349-368.

Oswald, R. F. (2001). Religion, family, and ritual: The production of gay, lesbian, bisexual, and transgender outsiders-within. *Review of Religious Research 43*(1), 39-50.

Pleck, E. (2000). *Celebrating the family: Ethnicity, culture, and family rituals.* Cambridge, MA: Harvard University Press.

Rappaport, R. (1979). *Ecology, meaning, and religion.* Berkeley, CA: North Atlantic Books.

Roberts, J. (1988). Setting the frame: Definitions, functions, and typology of rituals. In E. Imber-Black, J. Roberts, & E. Whiting (Eds.), *Rituals in families and family therapy.* New York: Norton.

Sherman, S. (1992). *Lesbian and gay marriage: Private commitments, public ceremonies.* Philadelphia: Temple University Press.

Smith, C. (1998). *American evangelicalism: Embattled and thriving.* Chicago: University of Chicago Press.

Taylor, V., & Whittier, N. (1992). Collective identity in social movement communities. In A. Morris & C. Mueller (Eds.), *Frontiers of social movement theory.* New Haven: Yale University Press.

Turner, V. (1969). *The ritual process: Structure and antistructure.* London: Routledge & Kegan Paul.

Turner, V. (1986). *The anthropology of performance.* New York: Performing Arts Journal Publications.

van Gennep, A. (1960). *The rites of passage* (M.B. Vizedom & G.L. Cafee, Trans.). Chicago: University of Chicago Press.

Wink, W. (1986). *Unmasking the powers: The invisible forces that determine human existence.* Philadelphia: Fortress Press.

Witham, L. (2000, August 7). Churches debate role of homosexual unions. *Insight on the News.*

Do Lesbians Change Their Last Names in the Context of a Committed Relationship?

Elizabeth A. Suter

Ramona Faith Oswald

SUMMARY. This exploratory study begins to redress a critical gap in the literature on committed same-sex relationships and last name practices. Data were gathered from an Internet survey, which included 16 lesbian respondents currently in a same-sex relationship. Analyses explored individual, couple, and family of origin factors associated with changing or not changing one's name. Name-changing was cited as a strategy for securing external recognition and acceptance of family status by outsiders. Not changing was cited as a strategy to preserve each partner's individual identity. Contrary to our expectations, changing one's last name was not associated with having a commitment ceremony. Instead, name-changing was ritualized on other occasions, special to the individual couple, such as an anniversary, a partner's birthday, or an intimate dinner party among friends. *[Article copies available for a fee from The Haworth Document Delivery Service: 1-800-HAWORTH. E-mail address: <docdelivery@haworthpress.com> Website: <http://www.HaworthPress.com> © 2003 by The Haworth Press, Inc. All rights reserved.]*

Address correspondence to: Dr. Elizabeth Suter, University of Nebraska-Lincoln, Department of Communication Studies, 439 Oldfather Hall, P.O. Box 880329, Lincoln, NE 68588-0329 (E-mail: esuter2@unl.edu).

[Haworth co-indexing entry note]: "Do Lesbians Change Their Last Names in the Context of a Committed Relationship?" Suter, Elizabeth A., and Ramona Faith Oswald. Co-published simultaneously in *Journal of Lesbian Studies* (Harrington Park Press, an imprint of The Haworth Press, Inc.) Vol. 7, No. 2, 2003, pp. 71-83; and: *Lesbian Rites: Symbolic Acts and the Power of Community* (ed: Ramona Faith Oswald) Harrington Park Press, an imprint of The Haworth Press, Inc., 2003, pp. 71-83. Single or multiple copies of this article are available for a fee from The Haworth Document Delivery Service [1-800-HAWORTH, 9:00 a.m. - 5:00 p.m. (EST). E-mail address: docdelivery@haworthpress.com].

KEYWORDS. Ritual, lesbian, naming practices, family of origin, couples

We wanted to try to do as many things as we could to make it clear that this is a family, including what legal things we could do. We changed our names in court primarily to have a legal record of this commitment.

–Kathleen Jensen

I like my last name because I feel it's a significant part of my identity. My name, in full, is who I am; it's how I know myself and, in turn, how others know. And it's all I have known. Changing it, or even altering my name, especially after so many years of calling and defining myself by one name, would be changing or even denying a part of who I know myself to be.

–Rebecca Larroquette

The study of names provides a window into how people accept or subvert concrete symbols of personhood, relationship status, and social position. Existing research has focused on whether or not heterosexual women change their last names upon marriage. No one has researched whether or not non-heterosexual people change their last names in the context of a committed relationship. Therefore, the purpose of our exploratory study is to begin documenting the naming practices of lesbian, gay, and bisexual (LGB) people. We do this using survey data collected from 16 lesbians. The questions that we seek to answer are: Do lesbians change their last names in the context of a committed relationship? What individual, couple, and family of origin factors are associated with changing or not changing? What are the reasons for changing or not changing?

REVIEW OF LITERATURE

Ninety percent of heterosexually married women in the United States take their husband's name upon marriage (Brightman, 1994; Johnson & Scheuble, 1995; Scheuble & Johnson, 1993; Scheuble, Klingemann, & Johnson, 2000). Seven key reasons have been found to explain why heterosexual women engage in this practice. One, they wanted to be conventional or honor tradition (Carbaugh, 1996; Foss & Edson, 1989; Kline, Stafford, & Miklosovic, 1996;

Suter, 2001; Twenge, 1997). Two, they wanted to create a family identity (Carbaugh, 1996; Foss & Edson, 1989; Kline, Stafford, & Miklosovic, 1996; Suter, 2001). Three, they wanted to change for individual identity reasons (Carbaugh, 1996; Kline, Stafford, & Miklosovic, 1996; Suter, 2001; Twenge, 1997). Four, they desired a good relationship with their husband (Foss & Edson, 1989; Fowler & Fuehrer, 1997). Five, they wished to avoid any confusion over the family membership of their children (Foss & Edson, 1989; Suter, 2001; Twenge, 1997). Six, they changed for practical reasons, such as confusion/simplicity or like/dislike of names (Foss & Edson, 1989; Kline, Stafford, & Miklosovic, 1996; Suter, 2001; Twenge, 1997). Seven, they expressed apathy or no reason (Foss & Edson, 1989; Twenge, 1997).

The majority of naming research has focused on the 10% of heterosexually married women who have deviated from the majority practice and chosen an alternative naming practice. Alternative practices are usually hyphenation, retaining one's own last name, or creating a new name for the couple. Four central reasons have been found to explain why these women have resisted convention and chosen an alternative naming practice. First, they wanted to maintain a previous ethnic, professional or family identity (Carbaugh, 1996; Foss & Edson, 1989; Fowler & Fuehrer, 1997; Kline, Stafford, & Miklosovic, 1996; Kupper, 1990; Twenge, 1997). Second, they felt that it would be easier to not change either because their husband's name was not appealing or because they did not want re-establish themselves with a new name (for example if they had published under their maiden name) (Carbaugh, 1996; Foss & Edson, 1989; Fowler & Fuehrer, 1997; Kline, Stafford, & Miklosovic, 1996; Kupper, 1990; Twenge, 1997). Third, they wanted to symbolize their equality within marriage (Foss & Edson, 1989; Fowler & Fuehrer, 1997; Kline, Stafford, & Miklosovic, 1996; Kupper, 1990). And, finally, they had an emotional bond with their name (Kline, Stafford, & Miklosovic, 1996; Kupper, 1990).

Our study extends previous work on naming practices by exploring whether or not and why lesbians change their last names in the context of committed same-sex relationships. In an attempt to conduct a literature review on the naming practices of committed same-sex couples, we searched indexes and databases in the fields of women's studies, linguistics, anthropology, sociology, communications, and psychology. This comprehensive search for information yielded no references pertaining to the topic of the naming practices of same-sex couples in committed relationships. We did find anecdotal references to naming practices in the context of studies about other topics of lesbian life. For example, Ellen Lewin's (1998) ethnography of same-sex commitment ceremonies includes two narratives in which two couples created a common last name due to plans to have children. The shared last name functioned as a symbol of their relationship with each other, and their relationship as parents to future children. Our exploratory study begins to redress this critical gap in the literature on committed same-sex relationships and last names. We examine which individual, couple, and family of origin factors are associated with changing or not changing one's name. We also document the reasons for changing or not changing.

METHODOLOGY

Data were collected from an Internet survey of 36 LGB respondents currently in a same-sex relationship. This paper uses a sub-sample of the 16 lesbians who responded to this survey. Fourteen of the lesbians were white, 1 African-American, and 1 Arab-American. All were in a same-sex relationship at the time of the survey. Relationships had lasted for an average of 9 years (ranged from 3-21 years, *SD* = 4 years).

Respondents were invited to complete a 3-part survey, which asked short answer and demographic questions, and invited them to provide a story about their last name. Surveys were returned privately to the first author in an e-mail message or via the U.S. mail.

The Survey

Respondents first indicated whether they had changed their last name in the context of their current same-sex relationship. Then they explained why they did or did not change their last name. If they had not changed their name, then they discussed whether or not they had considered doing so.

We then asked a series of questions about their current relationship, including: Do you cohabitate? Have you had a commitment ceremony? Have you taken steps to legalize your relationship? We hypothesized that cohabitation, legalization, and having a commitment ceremony would be associated with changing because they each suggest an interest in concretizing the couple's relationship. From this view, changing one's name would be an additional way to symbolically bolster the relationship.

Next, we asked respondents to rate on a scale from 1-5 how connected they felt to their immediate and extended families of origin, the LGB community, and LGB friends/acquaintances (higher values indicated higher degrees of connection). We also asked them to rate how much contact they had with their immediate and extended families of origin (1 = less than yearly, 2 = yearly, 3 = monthly, 4 = weekly, 5 = daily), the climate for them as a lesbian person within their immediate and extended families of origin (1 = hostile, 2 = tolerant, 3 =

supportive), and the number of lesbian, gay, or bisexual people within their families of origin (including themselves). We anticipated that less supportive relationships, less frequent contact with families of origin, and fewer LGB family members would be associated with name changing because respondents would be less attached to maintaining continuity with those ties. Further, we hypothesized that more connection with LGB people and community would be associated with not changing because doing so would be perceived as assimilating to heterosexual norms.

Finally, information was collected about their year of birth, race, annual income, and education. Age was calculated by subtracting year of birth from 2001. Income and education were measured ordinally. We anticipated that younger respondents would be more likely to change their names due to the more positive social climate in which they came out as compared to respondents who were part of the Stonewall or pre-Stonewall eras. We also hypothesized that respondents who changed would be less educated and have less income, which could indicate less attachment to a professional identity that might need to be maintained via keeping one's name.

Frequencies are reported in Table 1, where all reported values have been rounded up to whole numbers. Table 1 also summarizes our hypotheses.

Data Analysis

Naming status was correlated with the predicted quantitative variables. We also read the narratives supplied by respondents and tabulated the reasons that they offered for changing, not changing, or thinking about changing their names.

RESULTS

Four lesbians changed their last names in the context of their current committed same-sex relationship. Respondents who changed their last names were less educated and more connected to their parents and siblings. Name-changers were in less frequent contact with their parents and siblings, but more frequent contact with extended kin. There was a trend for name-changers to be younger. See Table 2 for correlation data.

All four name-changers sought to demonstrate family status to outsiders. This was expressed in a variety of ways, including, ". . . to establish publicly that we are a family" (Laura), or as a way to " . . . strengthen our presence as a couple, as a family" (Emily), or as Kathleen explained:

We took my last name because we wanted it to be clear that we were a family, and that any kids that joined us would be part of the family, too. We wanted our families of origin to be able to recognize this. So we went kind of traditional by taking my last name and keeping hers as a middle name for both of us. We both went to court to do it, to have the legal paper trail. My partner's court date turned out to be my birthday, so that was fun. We both went solemnly to court, she stood there and said her new name, then we went out for a nice dinner. Chocolate cake sealed the bargain.

TABLE 1. Descriptive Data and Hypotheses

Variable	H,	Frequency (N = 16)
CHANGED NAME?		25%
DEMOGRAPHICS		
Age	–	M = 37 years (SD = 7), Range = 25-52
Education	–	87% had an advanced degree, 13% had a BA
Income	–	Median category = $30,001 – $40K, Range = 0-$60K
PARTNER RELATIONSHIP		
Legalization	+	100%
Cohabitation	+	94%
Had a ceremony	+	50%
IMMEDIATE F of O		
Amount of contact	–	M = 4 (SD = 1), Range = 3-5
Connection	–	M = 2 (SD = 1), Range = 1-5
Climate	–	M = 2 (SD = 1), Range = 1-3
EXTENDED F of O		
Amount of contact	–	M = 2 (SD = 1), Range = 1-4
Connection	–	M = 3 (SD =1), Range = 1-5
Climate	–	M = 2 (SD = 1), Range = 1-3
# LGB in F of O	–	M = 2 (SD = 1), Range = 1-5
LGB CONNECTION		
To LGB individuals	–	M = 4 (SD = 1), Range = 2-5
To LGB community	–	M = 3 (SD = 1), Range = 2-5

H, = Hypothesized relationship to name changing

TABLE 2. Correlates of Name-Changing

Age	−.415+
Education	−.638*
Income	−.306
Legalization	--
Cohabitation	.149
Commitment ceremony	.000
Contact–immediate F of O	−.651*
Connected–immediate F of O	.607**
Climate–immediate F of O	−.355
Contact–extended F of O	.585*
Connected–extended F of O	.346
Climate–extended F of O	.275
# LGB in F of O	−.103
Connected–LGB individuals	.168
Connected–LGB community	.016

+ = p ≤ .10
* = p ≤ .05
** = p ≤ .001

Two parents cited a need for external others to recognize both partners as parents. For Laura and her partner, ". . . our main concerns were with making sure that the non-biological parent was going to be considered a parent by schools, doctors, etc. We also had some concern about my partner's family not viewing my biological child as part of their family. We decided to use my partner's last name as our family name when I was trying to biologically have kids. We figured that . . . giving a biological kid her last name . . . would also solve any confusion that could happen when a parent has a different last name from a child." For Kelly, "In particular, it was important to me as the biological mother that my children's names reflect that my partner is as clearly as much a parent that I am."

Two respondents changed in order to create distance from their families of origin. Emily, who survived an abusive family, explained: "When I met my partner and we realized our relationship would be permanent, it made sense to me to take her name. I like her family a lot–and taking her name made me feel like I was part of a sane, healthy family–and made us, as a couple, feel more like a family too." For Christine and her partner:

Our original plan was to do the hyphen thing . . . but we felt that it was too long. Then we were going to combine the names into something new and original. But nothing we came up with sounded right. Plus, we were working on this idea just around the time of the wedding. We found out just how unsupportive our families-of-origin really were of our relationship. We felt that since they didn't accept us as life partners and part of the family, we had no obligation to preserve their last name as part of our name. Plus, they really didn't deserve it. Sooo we came up with something original and that really represented us, and our love for each other.

Finally, one respondent created a new last name with her partner to demonstrate their love and commitment to each other. Christine explained, "My partner and I wanted to share a last name to reflect the fact that we got married/committed our life to each other. The last name is Spanish for penguins . . . penguins have become our family's symbol, and Spanish is a language we both love."

Of the 12 respondents that did not change their last names, 7 reported making a conscious decision to not change. Their reasons were as follows (numbers do not add up to 12 as respondents could provide more than one reason): Six did not change out of respect or like for their family of origin names and the history of those names. As Rebecca explained:

I recall seeing our family tree for the first time. I was amazed at how–after being unfolded several times–it spread across our dining room table. I remember seeing names I never heard before; learning (by parenthetical notations) when some early ancestors migrated from Wales to England, and when others immigrated from England to America; and knowing that some fought in the Revolutionary War, the Civil War, and the Great War . . . I recall tracing marriages, children, deaths. And, the most thrilling part, seeing the names I did not recognize fitting into this maze of interconnected relationships.

Four felt that their last name was an integral part of their identity. As Leslie said, " . . . I remain as I am, regardless of what relationship I am in." Similarly, for Pat changing her name for a relationship was not something she is willing to do, "Even if I were straight and legally married, I wouldn't change my name. My name is how the world and I have identified me for 30 years. It's part of my identity and I wouldn't change it because of a relationship."

Four were established in their careers and official records with their current last names. For Rebecca, "This has become more of an issue since developing a professional identity, where I use my full name on conference proposals, papers, article, etc. My name represents me in various forms, even if I'm not physically present." Susan summed up this influence, "I would be reluctant to do so [to change] largely for professional reasons–it would be a pain."

Three felt that name-changing was irrelevant to same-sex couples. As Sarah said, "I can't think of any compelling reason to change it. It's not like there's societal/family pressure for queers to change our names. The tradition for women to change their names to that of the man really only makes sense if there is a woman and a man." Jacqueline concurred, "I associate name changing with marriage."

Three did not like their partner's last name. Kelly did not change her name in large part because, " . . . my partner's name isn't as interesting as mine, and mine clearly reflects my ethnic heritage, which I am slightly more tuned into than she is to hers." Tracy was influenced not to change, " . . . because of the commonality of partner's name," while Susan did not change partly because, "My partner's last name is her ex-husband's last name, so hyphenating it would not be meaningful."

Three believed that keeping names separate would promote equality in their relationships. For example, as Anne said, " . . . it is important to my partner and I that we keep much of our lives separate. We have separate careers, separate friends, even separate belongings. Keeping separate names reflects our desire not to merge into a couple-being and to remain two separate individuals."

Two could not agree with their partners about what their new name should be. Tellu and her partner did not change, "mostly because we couldn't agree on what to change our names to." She later elaborated:

> I like my last name–it fits well with my first name (which is also Finnish)–and my partner likes hers. We couldn't agree to take each others (although we didn't try too hard), and changing them to a separate third name didn't meet either of our needs, but when we had children, it was clear we wanted them to reflect that we are all a family. . . . We talked about hyphenating our names as well, since their birth, but it feels cumbersome and we haven't had a good reason to do so yet. But it's a possibility in the future.

Finally, one respondent wanted to avoid the inconvenience of having to explain her name change to others. Camille did not change her name "to keep things easier. Society would not understand or accept this. It would be too difficult to explain at work, with friends, etc."

DISCUSSION

Though our study is exploratory and our results quite tentative, we cautiously suggest that lesbian naming practices constitute active negotiations with the idea of family membership at both family of origin and societal levels. This is in marked contrast with heterosexually married women who may take their family status for granted and be more concerned with upholding convention and pleasing their partners.

The seemingly odd finding that respondents who changed did so because they had a close connection but infrequent contact with parents and siblings may reflect complicated family relations between these respondents and their immediate families (see Laird, 1996; Weston, 1991). As Healy (1999) notes, decisions about how to verbalize lesbian relationships are based upon an assessment of whether verbal acknowledgement will be constructive. "Close connection" may refer to undesired enmeshment in a family drama that is dealt with by maintaining a physical distance. If this is true, then name-changing may function as a strategy to establish a symbolic distance that is consistent with the level of contact, and that affords a degree of independence from that drama. Alternatively, it is also possible that the felt sense of close connection to their parents and siblings may translate into an alignment with heteronormative norms and practices, such as name-changing.

In addition to internal family dynamics, naming practices may also constitute an attempt to claim family status at the societal level that is linked to being part of a post-Stonewall generation. Though only 25% of our respondents changed their last names, those that did tended to be younger. We suspect that younger lesbians are more likely to expect society to tolerate, if not support, them as family members. Interestingly, the 10% of heterosexual non-changers also tend to be younger. Though they have a different reference point with regards to family status than do lesbians who change their names, heterosexual non-changers may also expect society to tolerate if not support their choice even when it transgresses social norms. Future studies of naming should take generational differences into account, and should also attend to the ways in which lesbian and heterosexual experiences may be parallel.

We found it worthy of note that name-changing for the lesbians studied here was not associated with having a commitment ceremony. Despite the lack of correlation with having a commitment ceremony, we did find qualitative evidence that name changes were ritualized. For example, Kathleen and her partner ritualized their name change in a variety of unique ways. They celebrated their name change as part of their tenth anniversary. They then had the name change legalized, which meant a formal trip to the courthouse. The court date happened to fall on Kathleen's birthday. As a result, the legal name change was incorporated as part of Kathleen's birthday celebration ritual. Also, Emily, who changed her last name to her partner's, ritualized the change by formally announcing it at a dinner party for a group of their closest friends. Further, despite a lack of detail of a ritual provided, the specificity of Christine's response to the question, "At what point in your relationship did you change it?" suggests a ritual very easily might have accompanied the name change. Unlike others who generally answered this question in years, Christine specified, "23 months after meeting/starting to date and 5 months after our wedding." Even thought the heterosexual conflation of marriage and name-changing does not work for our lesbian respondents, they are creating rituals to mark the occasion. Laird (1988) posited that normative family rituals define women in relation to men, and encouraged clinicians to help women create new female-centered rituals. The ways in which lesbians do ritualize name-changing are worthy of future study, and may provide clinicians with models of female-centered ritual that can be adapted for family practice.

In addition to family, there may be social mobility issues impacting lesbian decisions to change or not change last names. Heterosexuals who break the norm for their social identity group and do not change have been found to be more highly educated (Brightman, 1994). By contrast, lesbians who broke the norm for their social identity group by changing were less educated. It is possible that this is simply a function of the fact that lesbians who changed were younger and less likely to have accumulated as much education as their elder counterparts. Professionalism may play a factor as well. For heterosexual women, the more established their career, the less inclined they are to change. It may further be the case then that younger lesbians are more willing to change their names because they have not established careers.

CONCLUSION

The results of this survey beg for future study of the naming practices of individuals in committed same-sex relationships as well as future study of how family of origin issues may influence these decisions. Our survey contributes to a growing body of literature that seeks to understand and document the lives of lesbian, gay, and bisexual individuals. Of the vast amount of literature published annually, only the smallest fraction is devoted to this task (Allen & Demo, 1995). One strategy for understanding the lives of LGB individuals is to look at how heteronormative practices, such as name-changing, are appropriated, rejected, and/or transformed.

This survey also contributes to the literature on ritual by integrating the perspective of individuals in committed same-sex relationships. The lack of connection between name-changing and a commitment ceremony is a marked difference from the naming practices of heterosexual women and warrants further exploration. One potentially enlightening avenue for further study is the unique ways in which lesbians do ritualize name-changing (albeit not as part of a commitment ceremony) and/or other practices that function as external symbols of their commitment to one another and status as a legitimate family form.

REFERENCES

Allen, K., & Demo, D. (1995). The families of lesbians and gay men: A new frontier in family research. *Journal of Marriage & the Family. 57*(1), 111-127.

Brightman, J. (1994, March). Why Hillary chooses Rodham Clinton. *American Demographics, 16*, 9-11.

Carbaugh, D. (1996). *Situating selves: The communication of social identities in American scenes.* Albany: State University of New York Press.

Foss, K., & Edson, B. (1989). What's in a name? Accounts of married women's name choices. *Western Journal of Speech Communication, 53*, 356-373.

Fowler, R. I., & Fuehrer, A. (1997). Women's marital names: An interpretive study of name retainers' concepts of marriage. *Feminism and Psychology, 7*, 315-320.

Healy, T. (1999). A struggle for language: Patterns of self-disclosure in lesbian couples. In J. Laird (Ed.), *Lesbians and lesbian families* (pp. 123-141). New York: Columbia University Press.

Johnson, D. R., & Scheuble, L. K. (1995). Women's marital naming in two generations: A national study. *Journal of Marriage and the Family, 57*, 724-732.

Kline, S. L., Stafford, L., & Miklosovic, J. C. (1996). Women's surnames: Decisions, interpretations and associations with relational qualities. *Journal of Social and Personal Relationships, 13*, 593-617.

Kupper, S. (1990). *Surnames for women: A decision-making guide.* Jefferson, NC: McFarland.

Laird, J. (1988). Women and ritual in family therapy. In E. Imber-Black, J. Roberts, & R. Whiting (Eds.), *Rituals in families and family therapy* (pp. 331-362). New York: W.W. Norton.

Laird, J. (1996). Invisible ties: Lesbians and their families of origin. In J. Laird & R.J. Green (Eds.), *Lesbians and gays in couples and families: A handbook for therapists* (pp. 89-122). San Francisco: Jossey Bass.

Lewin, E. (1998). *Ceremonies of lesbian and gay commitment: Recognizing ourselves.* New York: Columbia University Press.

Scheuble, L. K., & Johnson, D. R. (1993). Marital name change: Plans and attitudes of college students. *Journal of Marriage and the Family, 55*, 747-754.

Scheuble, L. K., Klingemann, K., & Johnson, D. R. (2000). Trends in women's marital name choices: 1966-1996, *Names, 48*, 105-114.

Stafford, L., & Kline, S. L. (1996). Married women's name choices and sense of self. *Communication Reports, 9*(1), 85-92.

Suter, E. (2001). *A community based study of married women's naming practices: Norms and traditions, individual identity, and meaning.* Unpublished doctoral dissertation, University of Illinois at Urbana-Champaign.

Twenge, J. M. (1997). "Mrs. his name": Women's preferences for married names. *Psychology of Women Quarterly, 21,* 417-429.

Weston, K. (1991). *Families we choose: Lesbians, gays, kinship.* New York: Columbia University Press.

Fear and Loathing in Mississippi:
The Attack on Camp Sister Spirit

Kate Greene

SUMMARY. In 1993, the small rural community of Ovett, Miss., and a group of self-described radical lesbian feminists clashed over the establishment by the women of a feminist educational retreat known as Camp Sister Spirit. This dispute took the form of physical and psychological harassment of the women, wide-open public debate in the community, in the press, and on television, federal mediation efforts, and two lawsuits. This article analyzes this dispute using Mary Daly's seven patterns of the sado-ritual syndrome (Daly, 1978). The analysis examines the ideological and moral standpoints of the participants, the issues of "blaming the victim" and scapegoating, the development of the conflict from a dispute between neighbors to the involvement of international media, national activists and the Clinton Administration, the transformation of the conflict from a political to legal dispute, the representations of the groups within the community and the media, the effect of public opinion on the dispute, and the politics of the media in the dispute. *[Article copies available for a fee from The Haworth Document Delivery Service: 1-800-HAWORTH. E-mail address: <docdelivery@haworthpress.com> Website: <http://www.HaworthPress.com> © 2003 by The Haworth Press, Inc. All rights reserved.]*

KEYWORDS. Ritual, lesbian, Camp Sister Spirit, Mary Daly, rural, feminism

Kate Greene is affiliated with the University of Southern Mississippi.
This article was previously published in *Women & Politics* 17(3) 1997.

[Haworth co-indexing entry note]: "Fear and Loathing in Mississippi: The Attack on Camp Sister Spirit." Greene, Kate. Co-published simultaneously in *Journal of Lesbian Studies* (Harrington Park Press, an imprint of The Haworth Press, Inc.) Vol. 7, No. 2, 2003, pp. 85-106; and: *Lesbian Rites: Symbolic Acts and the Power of Community* (ed: Ramona Faith Oswald) Harrington Park Press, an imprint of The Haworth Press, Inc., 2003, pp. 85-106. Single or multiple copies of this article are available for a fee from The Haworth Document Delivery Service [1-800-HAWORTH, 9:00 a.m. - 5:00 p.m. (EST). E-mail address: docdelivery@haworthpress.com].

In the summer of 1993, a small group of women, many of whom were lesbian, began the work of converting an old hog farm near Ovett, Miss., into Camp Sister Spirit, a feminist educational retreat. Shortly thereafter, a minor dispute between the women and their closest neighbor over access to the land escalated, and by the end of the year, the women were literally under siege from the citizens of Ovett who were opposed to a "lesbian retreat" in their community. Threats were made, shots were fired, fences were built, and the "culture war" was on in rural Mississippi.

The dispute between the women of Camp Sister Spirit and the citizens of Ovett is an ideological, political, and legal struggle that presents an excellent case study in any number of theoretical frameworks, e.g., social movements, conflict resolution, or civil rights (see Greene and Wheat, 1995). However, the interesting mix of a small Bible-belt community struggling against a smaller group of radical lesbian feminists suggested that a more unorthodox, non-traditional framework would provide an interesting analysis of this dispute. A framework which allows a unique analysis of the ideological, political, and legal aspects of this dispute is Mary Daly's patterns of the "sado-ritual syndrome" which she developed in *Gyn/Ecology* (1978) and used again in *Pure Lust* (1984).

Daly is a controversial figure among academic feminists, philosophers, and theologians. Among feminists she has been strongly criticized for her "essentialism," her failure to deal with racial, cultural, ethnic, national, class, and religious differences between women (Alcoff, 1988; Code, 1991; Hekman, 1990; Jaggar, 1983; Lorde, 1984; Spelman, 1988). Another criticism of Daly is that she is a conspiracy theorist. Since conspiracy theories do not have much value to political science because they ignore the institutional and systemic cause of oppression or repression, this is not an unreasonable criticism (Albert, 1992). Yet, without conceding that Daly is a conspiracy theorist, the fact that her analysis of patriarchal forms of oppression against women even hints at conspiracy theory may be why her framework seems so appropriate for this particular dispute. Because the sado-ritual grows out of deep underlying misogyny, the analysis is appropriate in a context of a politics of hate and fear which is clearly at work in Ovett, Miss. The attack on the women of Camp Sister Spirit had its roots in both misogyny and homophobia and found much of its support from the radical right, which is also known for rhetoric involving conspiracy theory.

In *Gyn/Ecology* (1978), Daly noted that the most explicit oppression of women has been perpetrated through a variety of "barbarous" rituals such as Indian suttee, African female genital mutilation, Chinese foot-binding, European witch burning and American gynecology. She analyzed these rituals in terms of the basic patterns they had in common and she named these patterns the "sado-ritual syndrome" (1978, 111). The "sado-ritual syndrome" contains seven patterns:

1. The sado-ritual syndrome begins with an obsession with purity.
2. There is a total erasure of responsibility for the atrocities performed through such rituals.
3. Ritual practices have an inherent tendency to "catch on" and spread.
4. Women are used as scapegoats and token torturers.
5. The syndrome includes a compulsive orderliness, obsessive repetitiveness, and fixation upon minute detail, which divert attention from the horror.
6. Behavior which at other times and places is unacceptable becomes acceptable and even normative as a consequence of conditioning through the ritual.
7. There is a legitimation of the rituals by the rituals of "objective scholarship" despite appearances of disapproval (Daly, 1978, 131-133).

Although Daly's analysis in *Gyn/Ecology* was applied to large-scale religious, cultural, and institutional rituals, the patterns she identified are not confined to these forms of oppression. The patriarchal struggle to keep women oppressed repeats these patterns in the smaller, often isolated battles lived out each day in real time by real women. Indeed, in *Pure Lust* (1984), Daly applies this analysis to horizontal violence within women's groups (67-72).

As noted above, this framework is not an orthodox or traditional political science framework, but it still addresses traditional political science questions and issues. For example, the first pattern notes that the "syndrome begins with an obsession with purity." In general terms, this pattern permits the identification of the basic ideological and moral standpoints of the participants. The second pattern, which deals with the erasure of responsibility for the ritual behavior, addresses the issue of "blaming the victim" so often evidenced in feminist concerns and now present in much of the right wing rhetoric. The third pattern, "an inherent tendency to spread," provides an opportunity to trace the development of this conflict from a mere dispute among neighbors to the involvement of national and international media, national activists, and the Clinton Administration, as well as its transformation from a political to a legal dispute. The fourth pattern permits an examination of the roles of oppositional women in this conflict and the use of scapegoating as a political strategy. The fifth pattern presents an opportunity to analyze the strategies of both sides to influence their opposition's representations within the community and in the media. The sixth pattern involves an analysis of the general climate of public opinion in the community involved in the dispute and how that climate affected political and social action. Finally, the last pattern invokes an examination of the media's political role in the dispute. These are eclectic concerns and analyses, but the result is greater understanding of this dispute.

THE ESTABLISHMENT OF CAMP SISTER SPIRIT

Brenda and Wanda Henson, a lesbian couple from Gulfport, Miss., are the organizers and representatives of a non-profit charitable, organization known as Sister Spirit Incorporated (hereafter Sister Spirit). According to the Hensons, Sister Spirit is an all-volunteer organization dealing with social issues such as racism, sexism, family violence, homophobia, hunger, job equity, and housing (Greene, 8 January 1994). The volunteers are primarily, but not exclusively, women and include women from all walks of life.

For several years, the Hensons ran a feminist bookstore known as Southern Wild Sisters Unlimited. Sister Spirit grew out of the bookstore experience when the Hensons found themselves serving as an informational resource for the local lesbian and feminist community. After having to provide emergency housing for battered lesbians who were turned away from a local shelter, the Hensons created Sister Spirit. In addition to serving as a resource, Sister Spirit established a food bank, a clothes closet for displaced homemakers, worked with the Star Literacy Center on the Gulf Coast and sponsored workshops on issues such as self-esteem and racism. In addition, Sister Spirit organized drug- and alcohol-free activities for the lesbian community on the Gulf Coast, including the Gulf Coast Womyn's Festival. Sister Spirit also established a mission to Isla Mujeres off Cancun, Mexico which provides clothes, medical supplies, and toys to a colony of Maya Indians through a Mexican Red Cross Outpost.

In July 1993, Sister Spirit purchased, for $60,000, a rundown 120 acre hog farm near the rural community of Ovett. Ovett is a poor, unincorporated community in south Jones County, 25 miles northeast of Hattiesburg. The approximately 250 citizens are primarily small farmers, small businesspersons, or employed by nearby small industry, and the vast majority are Christian, many of whom are fundamentalists. The town itself consists of a local general store, a post office, and a gas station. According to the Hensons, the purchase of the land was an important step toward a goal long sought by the Hensons, the creation of a feminist educational and cultural retreat and a safe haven for the Gulf Coast Womyn's Festival. The land was named Camp Sister Spirit (Greene, 8 January 1994).

By August 1993, the Hensons and approximately 20 other women began creating Camp Sister Spirit out of the brush, woods, and the six buildings on the land: a house-like structure, a barn, and four hog barns. Each of these required extensive renovation. During the early days on the land, the women had their first encounter with their neighbor, Ray Tucker, who was a friend of Walter Bailey, Jr., the previous owner of the land. Bailey had not lived on the land for some time, although some old farming equipment remained and Tucker and other neighbors used the farm as a hunting camp. According to the Hensons, Bailey had 30 days to remove any equipment he wanted from the land. At Bailey's request, Tucker removed several pieces of equipment during that time, but he did not remove an old tractor which was clearly in disrepair. On the thirty-second day, Tucker requested access to the land to get the tractor, but he was told that he was no longer free to come onto the land and that he should have Bailey discuss the removal of the tractor with the Hensons. According to Wanda Henson, the deal was formally closed a month later and because Bailey made no mention of the tractor, the women believed that it was theirs to repair and use (Greene, 16 January 1994).

All seemed to be going well on the land until early November, the start of hunting season, when the women discovered a female puppy shot through the stomach and draped over the mailbox. Two days later the camp started receiving phone calls from men asking if they were lesbians and if they "rented out women" or "sold women." On November 12, 1993, the local television station, WDAM, informed Brenda that it had received an anonymous letter containing a copy of Sister Spirit's newsletter *The Grapevine*. WDAM informed Brenda Henson that copies of this newsletter were being distributed at local churches and businesses in the areas surrounding the Camp. Brenda Henson granted an interview with WDAM, which aired a piece emphasizing not the purpose of the camp, or the activities of Sister Spirit, but the fact there were lesbians on the land.

By the end of November, the harassing phone calls to Camp Sister Spirit escalated and a woman called and told the camp to "expect the KKK to burn a cross on you." According to the Hensons, the local Christian ministers association publicly announced that they would be watching the camp for "immoral activity." On the 28th of November, the *Hattiesburg American*, a local newspaper, published a column by a citizen of Ovett, J. D. Hendry. Hendry attacked the women on the issue of their lesbianism. Using excerpts from the newsletter, Hendry painted the camp as a haven for "every stray lesbian in the country" and suggested that these immoral, man-hating women intended to recruit the wives and daughters of Ovett into lesbianism (Hendry, 28 November, 1993). He called for a town meeting to discuss ways of removing Camp Sister Spirit from the land. The meeting was held on December 6, 1993, in the Ovett Community Center.

Locally, the *Hattiesburg American* began publishing letters to the editor and op-ed pieces both in favor of and against Camp Sister Spirit. The stream of letters continued for several months. Soon the Camp Sister Spirit story began to trickle out into the national media. Short pieces on the dispute were aired on CNN and NBC and an article was published in *Newsweek* (Turque et al., 1993). In December, Sister Spirit and the leaders of the Ovett group (J. D. Hendry, Paul Walley, and John Allen) appeared on the *Oprah Winfrey Show*. This was the first time that both sides met face-to-face. The show aired on December 21, 1993, and while it did nothing to advance or resolve the dispute, it gave the Hensons and the leaders of the Ovett group an opportunity to clearly present their case.

Just before taping the *Oprah Winfrey Show*, Hendry and the "camp opponents" asked the Jones County Board of Supervisors to make recommendations regarding the type of legal action the group might be able to take against the Camp (James, 21 December 1993). They also asked the supervisors to force the retreat to disclose its federal grant work and/or tax-exempt status. The supervisors voted unanimously to ask the county attorney to research the matter. On January 3, 1994, the residents of Ovett met at the Jones County Courthouse in Ellisville to discuss ways to shut down Camp Sister Spirit. By this time, the national and international media had arrived in Ovett. In Ovett were correspondents for the *Village Voice*, *The Washington Post*, *The Manchester Guardian*, and ABC's newsmagazine *20/20*. According to local news accounts, 350 residents attended this meeting (although Ovett is reported to be a community of 200) (James, 4 January 1994). Hendry announced that a lawsuit would be filed against Camp Sister Spirit. Money was also collected for the "Ovett Community Defense Fund." The following day the Jones County Board of Supervisors informed the Ovett group that the Board had no authority to "invade a lesbian group's right to live on its own property" and rejected the group's demand that the board investigate Sister Spirit's federal tax status and use of federal funds (James, 5 January 1994).

Throughout this time, the threats and harassment of the women continued and even escalated. Christmas night the women received a death threat over the phone. On December 30, 1993, a group of women at the camp reported being intentionally fired upon by unknown individuals. The sheriff's deputy dismissed their claim saying that it was probably just the sounds of local hunters in the area. On January 5, 1994, several calls to a local radio call-in show also threatened the women with violence. Later that week, someone spiked the driveway of the camp resulting in the destruction of two sets of vehicle tires. On January 13, 1994, the camp received another bomb threat through the mail. At this point the FBI finally assigned an agent to investigate the harassment of the women (Remwolt, 15 January 1994).

On February 18, U.S. Attorney General Janet Reno, responding to a petition by the National Gay and Lesbian Task Force (NGLTF), announced that she was authorizing the FBI to investigate the threatening letter mailed to the camp. Reno also authorized the Community Relations Service of the U.S. Department of Justice to mediate a compromise in the dispute between the Camp and the Ovett group, now known as Mississippi for Family Values (MFV) (McLaurin, 19 February 1994).

On March 5, 1994, MFV held a fund-raiser at a local public elementary school which was attended by approximately 200 citizens (McLaurin, 6 March 1994). The fund-raiser was to support the lawsuit that the citizens group had been threatening to file. Before suing the camp, however, the group sued Janet Reno in the U.S. District Court. According to the group's lawyer, Mike Barefield, the suit charged that Reno had no authority to mediate the dispute through the Community Relations Service, thus violating the Ninth and Tenth Amendments to the Constitution, and that Reno had violated MFV's First Amendment right to free speech (Maute, 7 March 1994). On March 19, 1994, the MFV and the Department of Justice signed a consent decree where MFV agreed to drop the suit against Janet Reno, and the Community Relations Service ended attempts at mediation (Braswell, 19 March 1994). Finally, on March 22, 1994, 11 neighbors with land adjoining the camp sought an injunction in the Chancery Court of Jones County against the building of the retreat under Mississippi's common law private nuisance.

In May, MFV held another fund-raiser (Maute, 15 May 1994) and minor incidents of harassment, such as the dumping of a dead skunk at the gate, continued to occur. The Hensons reported that throughout April and May their neighbors were regularly firing multiple rounds of ammunition just across the boundary lines of the camp. Tucker reportedly allowed his friends to set up a firing range just at the edge of the camp and another neighbor admitted to having fired over 80 rounds from a semi-automatic assault rifle on a single occasion. The firing of weapons was a strategy used against the women from early on in the dispute (Greene, 31 May 1994). However, over the Memorial Day weekend, the 6th Annual Gulf Coast Womyn's Festival was held at the camp without incident.

On July 6, 1994, a Congressional hearing, chaired by Barney Frank, D-MA and Jerry Nadler, D-NY, of the House Judiciary Subcommittee on Civil and Constitutional Rights, was held in Jackson, Miss. The hearing was to determine if the state and local officials had adequately protected the residents of the camp and if there was a need for federal legislation if the local officials were not protecting the women's rights (Christensen, 30 June 1994; Maute, 6 July 1994). In addition to the women, Hendry and John Allen, a local minister, testified. Jones County Sheriff Maurice Hooks and the deputy who patrols the

Ovett area were also asked to testify but did not appear. Mississippi Congress-man Mike Parker, a supporter of the Ovett citizens group, objected to the hearing saying that it was "about land use and a local matter" and "a waste of taxpayer's money" (Maute, 6 July 1994).

On May 19, 1995, the case finally went to trial. The plaintiff's argued that the camp would be detrimental to their peaceful residential community (most of the neighbors are farmers by trade) by increasing traffic flow and noise. No mention was made of the women's lesbianism, though the plaintiffs did attempt to make themselves out as the victims of a national conspiracy by gays to use Ovett to advance their cause and as the true victims of harassment. In July 1995, Judge Frank McKenzie ruled against MFV and held that camp Sister Spirit could be used as a retreat. In his opinion McKenzie held that if he was to issue an injunction against the gathering of women at the camp then he would also have to issue injunctions against large church gatherings, political rallies, family reunions and even gatherings of deer hunters (Maute, 23 May 1995). Although MFV threatened to appeal, there was none, and the Hensons returned to their work (Slaton, 6 July 1995).

THE PATTERNS OF THE SADO-RITUAL SYNDROME

Because the events surrounding the spooking of Camp Sister Spirit are not ritualistic in the same way that Chinese foot-binding and African genital mutilation were ritualistic, the analysis that follows will not attempt to treat the events as though it were a ritual. The significance of the patterns is that they suggest an unique analysis of the politics of this dispute.

Pattern #1: The Sado-Ritual Begins with an Obsession with Purity

The obsession with purity is the most obvious pattern present in the dispute surrounding the establishment of Camp Sister Spirit because it is evidenced in the ideological and moral beliefs of the leaders of the Ovett citizens group. Whether in the newspaper, on the *Oprah Winfrey Show*, or at the congressional hearing, both Hendry, the primary spokesman, and Allen, a local minister, continually emphasized the right of the Ovett community to keep out "undesirable," "immoral," and "abominable" influences. Both meetings of the Ovett citizens ignored the service activities of the women and focused on the issue of homosexuality (James, 4 January 1994). A film, distributed nationally by the Christian Coalition and Traditional Values Coalition, was shown at the second meeting. This film echoed most of the citizens views on homosexuality: that it is a sin and an abomination before God, that gays and lesbians are depraved and sick, that they spread disease (AIDS), and that they are predators on the weak and innocent. In one article, Hendry was quoted as saying, "This group is seeking out and recruiting women. . . . They have a sign outside their camp saying 'No men allowed.' We're not used to that kind of thing around here" (Remwolt, 6 December 1993). Allen repeatedly referred to Ovett as a "rural . . . family values . . . religious (Christian) community" that is being "invaded" and threatened with the possibility of becoming "a hub of homosexual activity." Allen argued that communities that tolerate homosexuals and homosexual activities are destined to be overtaken by hordes of homosexuals and Ovett had a right to defend itself against such an assault. Camp Sister Spirit is thus viewed as a threat to the purity of Ovett as a "rural . . . family values . . . religious community."

In addition to the purity of the community as a whole, Hendry and Allen also expressed concern for the heterosexual and patriarchal purity of the "wives and daughters" of Ovett. According to these men, the social/charity work of the women of Camp Sister Spirit was nothing more than a means for infiltrating a community, giving them access to the local "wives and daughters" to seduce them into lesbianism (Allen, 1994; Hendry, 1993; Shows, 1993). The concern of these men was probably not simply that their wives and daughters would be seduced into lesbianism, but that the women of Camp Sister Spirit would encourage the women to get an education, perhaps even a job, or give them the strength and means to leave abusive relationships, thereby threatening patriarchal dominance (Greene, September 21, 1994). The Hensons reported that it was not long after the dispute became public that several local women called them asking for help in leaving abusive relationships.

At the congressional hearing, Hendry even alleged that the camp was "polluting" the drinking water of Ovett by dumping raw sewage into the local water supply. While the camp had difficulty hiring a contractor to install a septic system because the local contractors received threats regarding work for the camp, a septic system was eventually installed (Greene, 6 July 1994). The accusation, of course, was intended to further frighten and anger the citizens of Ovett and increase the fear and hatred they already had of the women.

This obsession with maintaining the patriarchal, heterosexual purity of Ovett shows the degree to which the people of Ovett differ ideologically from the women of Camp Sister Spirit. Ovett is an "island community" composed primarily of Christian men and women who apparently support the notion of traditional family structures, patriarchal dominance, and Biblical moral values to a much greater degree than most Americans (Greene and Wheat, 1995, 325). The Hensons, on the other hand, are another island community on the edge of the island community of Ovett. Ideologically the women of Camp Sister Spirit are radical lesbian feminists who support a multitude of family structures, seek to eliminate patriarchal dominance, and live according to feminist rather than Biblical moral values. Both sides are outsiders, but in opposing directions from the mainstream. Thus, the ideological threat to each other is exaggerated. The Ovett citizens group felt it was being invaded by godless heathens with a sinful agenda and Camp Sister Spirit felt it was having to defend itself against the Bible-toting patriarchs' continual efforts to subvert its mission of educating women. In terms of each achieving the "good and moral life," they are each their greatest obstacle.

Pattern #2: There Is a Total Erasure of Responsibility for the Atrocities Performed Through Such Rituals

The primary tool for erasing the responsibility for the atrocities of Chinese foot-binding, Indian *suttee*, and African genital mutilation is to shift the responsibility to women. This is done by creating a situation where women themselves perform the sado-ritual upon their daughters or there is some type of "blaming the victim." In Ovett, there has been much effort put into blaming the victim. Harvey Shows stated in an op-ed piece in the *Hattiesburg American* that the women had "goaded" the people of Ovett into harassing them by moving into Ovett and stealing a tractor (26 December 1993). It was suggested that the women purposefully selected Ovett because they somehow knew the citizens of Ovett would respond negatively, thus assuring national news coverage to advertise their "gay agenda." According to Wanda Henson, it was even suggested at the trial that the Hensons leaked their newsletter in an effort to inflame the community (Greene, 21 May 1995).

Another way that Ovett attempted to erase the responsibility for the harassment was to claim that none of it happened, that the women were simply making it up. Sheriff Hooks, the Jones County Sheriff, reportedly claimed that the women started the entire dispute themselves by killing the puppy that was found on the mailbox or that it had been hit by a car and the women used the opportunity to accuse their neighbors (Greene, 21 September 1994). At the trial, the MFV lawyer insisted there was no gunshot in the puppy (Maute, 23 May 1995).

As Daly notes, blaming the victim is a strategy that has long been used against women in the sado-rituals, and it continues to be used today in feminist efforts to address rape and domestic violence. It was also a strategy used against blacks during the civil rights movements. Indeed, one of the camp's neighbors compared the Hensons to Emmitt Till in his testimony at the Congressional hearings (Lee, 31 July 1994). Ricky Cole, neighbor to the camp and one of the original plaintiffs in the nuisance suit, admitted that the neighbors of the camp were indeed engaging in a campaign of harassment with the intent of scaring the women away, but he insisted that the Hensons brought the harassment upon themselves. Cole noted: "Emmitt Till didn't expect to be killed for whistling at a white woman. These ladies most probably didn't expect to have the vicious response that they got. But when you walk through the graveyard, you ought to whistle" (Lee, 31 July 1994).

Pattern #3: Ritual Practices Have an Inherent Tendency to "Catch On" and Spread

Daly noted that rituals tend to spread from the patriarchal elites to the upwardly aspiring lower echelons (1978, 132). This trend has been somewhat evidenced in the actual physical and psychological harassment of the women, though the trend may be based more on age than economic or social status. The initial problems began with the camp's actual neighbors, but once Hendry and the others made the dispute public, the harassment spread to local youth, usually drunken young men, who physically trespassed on the land. Even the local school bus stopped at the gate and the children would yell "faggot" at the women. The number of harassment incidents also seemed to be connected to the amount of media attention received. When the media attention died down in the spring of 1994, most of the harassment occurred only when the women went into town or it came from close neighbors of the camp. After each new fund-raiser and the Congressional hearings, however, new incidents by young men increased.

Yet, more important than the way the harassment of the women spread in the Ovett community was the development of the dispute from a local controversy to one which involved the national media, the intervention of the Justice Department, and Congressional hearings. As noted above, the citizens of Ovett and others suggested that the women came to Ovett seeking publicity and that this dispute was a "conspiracy" on the part of the national gay and lesbian organizations who bought the land and recruited the Hensons and other caretakers in order to force changes in federal laws (Greene, 21 September 1994; Maute, 18 May 1995). Yet the citizens' group of Ovett were mostly responsible for the local and national publicity surrounding the dispute. The women of the camp did not announce to the community or their neighbors that they or many of their volunteers were lesbians. According to the Hensons, their strategy was to blend into the community slowly and gain the trust and respect of their neighbors so that if their lesbianism became known, the neighbors would consider it irrelevant (Greene, 13 September 1994). Their lesbianism was only discovered by the community when the camp newsletter was anonymously distributed. J. D. Hendry of Ovett also published the first op-ed piece in the

Hattiesburg American (28 November 1993), sparking a long community debate through letters to the editor and op-ed pieces.

Interestingly, the citizens of Ovett may not have originated the idea to organize around the issue. While Hendry suggested in his op-ed piece that Ovett oppose the camp, the first organized opposition meeting was called by a Jackson, representative of the Southern Baptist Convention, Paul Jones. Jones was the first to suggest political action to stop the construction of the camp when he suggested that the citizens group "forc[e] the county Board of Supervisors to use laws that allow the Board to approve the use of incorporated land" (Braswell, 7 December 1993). Thus, the Ovett group, at the instigation of others, were also the first to involve local government officials.

All this time, the Hensons and their lawyer were writing letters to their neighbors hoping to put a stop to the harassment informally by countering the misinformation and innuendo being spread through the local media. When it became clear that the Ovett group was dedicated to removing the women from the land and the harassment continued, the Hensons appeared on a public affairs program on WLOX, a Mississippi Gulf Coast television station. The Hensons felt that their physical safety required visibility (Greene, 21 September 1994), so their turn to the media was a defensive measure, while the Ovett group used the media as an offensive measure to attack the women. The *Oprah Winfrey Show* was attended by both sides with at least 40 Ovett citizens making the trip to Chicago to be in the audience. Hendry's mother also appeared on the *Jerry Springer* and *Rolanda* talk shows. Neither side shied away from national publicity (James, 15 December 1993; 17 December 1993; Maute, 11 December 1993; Powers, 17 January 1994).

The Ovett group also quickly made political connections with national religious right organizations such as Christian Coalition, the Traditional Values Coalition, and the American Family Association as was evidenced at the second meeting by the showing of the anti-gay video. Paul Walley, an attorney who occasionally served as an opposition spokesman, also appeared on Pat Buchanan's radio talk show. The Hensons countered by doing an interview for National Public Radio and seeking assistance from the NGLTF. The Ovett group's name, Mississippi for Family Values, was based on Colorado for Family Values, the group that organized the anti-gay amendment in Colorado (Lee, 31 July 1994).

Following the second Ovett meeting was an intense period of harassment, including several death threats. It was a death threat through the mail that brought in the involvement of the FBI and a petition from the NGLTF and letters from national civil rights leaders that led Attorney General Reno to send mediators from the Community Relations Service. The Hensons felt that there was no reason to mediate their constitutional rights, but willingly met with the representatives. The Ovett group responded to this gesture by refusing to meet with the mediators and suing the Attorney General for allegedly violating their rights of free speech and some unspecified 10th Amendment violation, thus generating more publicity (Maute, 7 March 1994).

With regard to Congressional attention, Representative Mike Parker (R-MS) supported the opposition group in the press and in public when he attended and spoke at a fund-raiser for MFV (Maute, 15 May 1994). The hearings held by Representatives Frank and Nadler were intended to examine the question of whether civil rights legislation was needed to protect gays and lesbians (Maute, 6 July 1994). It was another opportunity for the women of Sister Spirit to describe the harassment they had been experiencing, but it also provided the opposition with a forum to publicly express its opposition to the camp and large numbers of Ovett citizens made the trip to Jackson (Maute, 7 July 1994).

The dispute between Ovett and the Camp was also transformed from a political to a legal debate at the instigation of the Ovett group. Eleven (eventually five) of the camp's neighbors filed suit in state court against the camp using the common law of private nuisance to seek an injunction prohibiting the use of the land as a "lesbian" retreat. It was also MFV that sued Janet Reno in federal court for sending mediators from the Community Relations Service of the Department of Justice.

The strategy of using nuisance law against the camp seemed unlikely to be a notion conceived by the Ovett group, but Paul Walley claimed to get the idea from a funeral home case he recalled from a law school moot court competition. Nuisance laws against gay establishments, particularly bars, have long been used as a way of preventing gay men and lesbians from congregating (Rubenstein, 1993, 209). States sought to prevent gays and lesbians from gathering together because it was there where gays and lesbians began to gain a sense of community, a sense of political consciousness, and where the gay rights movement eventually began. The use of nuisance suit against the Camp, then, is not without precedent.

Yet, once the case went to trial, the rhetoric of the neighbors and opposition suddenly changed from its hate rhetoric to one of family and property issues. According to Barefield, "They oppose the camp, not because of the [lesbian] lifestyles, but because of the noise and traffic in the area" (Maute, 19 May 1995). This is in direct contrast to all the prevailing rhetoric which insisted that it was the women's lesbianism that they opposed. Indeed, when Walley first suggested the notion of using nuisance law on the "Buchanan and Company" radio show, he opposed the retreat because it "represented things in opposition to Ovett community standards."

Pattern #4: Women Are Used as Scapegoats or Token Torturers

While the leadership of the citizens group and the primary spokespersons against the camp were men, Ovett women and others from the surrounding area wrote letters to the editor of the *Hattiesburg American* against the camp and openly opposed the camp on the talk and news shows. Much of the rhetoric coming from these women was biblical and echoed the rhetoric of John Allen, the fundamentalist minister. They opposed the camp because lesbianism is a sin. Because they support the biblical command that women are to be subservient to their husbands, these women also criticized feminism and feminists as being un-Christian. Other women who spoke against the camp spoke as mothers and expressed fear for their children and themselves.

One curious piece in the *Laurel Leader-Call* suggested that the way to deal with the camp was to send in "our women":

> So my solution is simply to get in the game with our best players, our women. Let's accept their invitation to visit their retreat and learn the ways of feminism and lesbianism. Let's send a few bus loads of "steel magnolias" in there and watch the fur fly.
>
> I'd love to be a fly on the wall as the sisters try to "re-educate" about 30 members of the Laurel Junior Auxiliary. Or let's send a circle a week, from each church in Jones County to be taught the virtues of lesbianism. Can you imagine who would be teaching whom? Why, within six weeks we'd be running engagement announcements for the sisters. Our womenfolk, the pride of the South, will have quietly dismantled the camp. (Barrett, 28 December 1993)

It is rare when men so openly identify their strategy to use women as "token torturers" to do their bidding.

Yet, more interesting than using local women to attack the camp is the wholesale use of scapegoating by MFV. According to Sklar (1995) and Berlet (1994), scapegoating has become a widespread national phenomenon with regard to the economic system and "talk-show demagogues have built their careers on a rising volume of hate." The poor, women, blacks, gays and lesbians, and programs such as affirmative action and AFDC are being blamed for the economic woes of white men and the result has been significant political success for the far right. In Mississippi's cultural climate and with MFV's connections to the religious right, it is not surprising that MFV put a great deal of effort into a strategy of demonizing and scapegoating the caretakers of Camp Sister Spirit. They represented the women as sinners, as predators seeking to "seduce" women and (girl) children into lesbianism, as liars, as thieves, as polluters of their drinking water, as man-haters and as supporters of the "militant homosexual agenda." At every opportunity, Allen accused the women of supporting NAMBLA, a national pedophile organization.

The Ovett group even distorted the value of the women's social service activities by claiming that these were a pretense allowing them to "infiltrate" an unsuspecting community. The social service work of the women virtually disappeared from the rhetoric of the dispute despite the Hensons' attempts to emphasize it. In addition, when the women started a new food bank at the camp, they found that while the people of nearby Ellisville were willing to accept their services, no Ovett resident would avail themselves of it. If the residents of Ovett, and particularly the neighbors of the camp, saw these women as such terrible beings, it was easy to justify both the harassment and the legal efforts to shut down the camp as a retreat.

Pattern #5: The Syndrome Includes a Compulsive Orderliness, Obsessive Repetitiveness, and Fixation upon Minute Detail, Which Divert Attention from the Horror

The constant repetition of particular characterizations of the players in this dispute undoubtedly served the purpose of diverting attention away from the real issue: whether Sister Spirit could establish a feminist educational retreat on private property. The idea of women being able to exercise control over their own property was lost under the barrage of attacks on lesbianism and its perceived threat to the community and the camp's defense against these attacks. The obsession of the Ovett group with lesbianism has already been extensively discussed above. The representation of the people of Ovett by the women of Camp Sister Spirit and the media, however, also deserves attention.

The people of Ovett clearly felt that they were being portrayed by the media as "hate mongers and hicks" (Shows, 1993), men on a witch-hunt (James, 15 December 1993), and "intolerant bigots" (Sanford, 6 March 1994). An examination of the news coverage shows that the local media usually just allowed the people of Ovett to speak for themselves, but many letters to the editors accused the Ovett group of being intolerant and "un-Christian." Janet Reno criticized them for intolerance and bigotry in her letter authorizing the mediation by the Community Relations Service (McLaurin, 19 February 1994). The Hensons referred to the Ovett group as an "opposition hate group" and as "terrorists." The women of the camp often described their situation in militaristic terms; that is, they were "under attack" by the religious right or "under siege" by their neighbors, supporting a view of the opposition as violent (Faggart, 1993; Fortenberry, 6 March 1994; Tisdall, 1993; and unsigned, 11 January 1994).

The national media was much more likely to present the story in these terms than the local papers. With the exception of the reference to MFV as terrorists on a computer bulletin board, the women of Camp Sister Spirit did not strategically resort to scapegoating or the use of hate rhetoric. The opposition did accuse the women of reciprocal harassment, however, at the Congressional hearings and at the trial (Maute, 23 May 1995). One woman in Laurel, Miss., was arrested for harassing J. D. Hendry, but no connection between the woman and the camp was ever made (James, 25 March 1994). At the hearing, Hendry also played several "obscene" messages he had received on his answering machine. At the trial, Hendry again attempted to make himself out as the victim of harassment (Maute, 23 May 1995). None of this harassment was directly traceable to the camp, and the women denied they encouraged such behavior in the same way that MFV argued that it did not support or encourage the harassment against Camp Sister Spirit.

Pattern #6: Behavior Which at Other Times and Places is Unacceptable Becomes Acceptable and Even Normative as a Consequence of Conditioning Through the Ritual

The sixth pattern suggests the need for an analysis of the general climate of public opinion in the community involved in the dispute and how that climate affected political and social action. The fact that drunken young men felt free to trespass on the women's land and that school children were encouraged by their bus driver to shout "faggot" at the women suggests that the climate of public opinion in Ovett and Jones County was fiercely against the women and strongly supportive of expressions of homophobia. Indeed, one young man in nearby Laurel felt that the homophobia was so strong and so acceptable that he could kill two gay men and get away with it. Indeed, his boasting about the crime resulted in his arrest and conviction (Bundy, 13 October 1994). In Ovett itself, the Hensons reported that they had received some support from their neighbors and others in Ovett, but most were afraid to be open in their support because they feared retaliation from their neighbors (Greene, 6 July 1994). Also, the Hensons had difficulty finding individuals or companies who would provide services because of threats received by the providers from the Ovett opposition.

The strength of anti-lesbian and anti-gay feeling in the area is also evident in the lack of public support for Camp Sister Spirit by the local lesbian and gay community. There is no organized lesbian or gay community in Hattiesburg, the largest city near Ovett. While a few local lesbians and gay men assisted in the construction of the camp or provided monetary assistance, for the most part the local lesbians and gay men were silent. In private conversations with the writer, some even criticized the Hensons for choosing Ovett or for their handling of the dispute. There was more support from the gay and lesbian community on the Mississippi Gulf Coast than from the Hattiesburg or Laurel communities, and there was limited support from the Jackson, lesbian and gay group.

The local lesbian and gay community has probably remained silent for two reasons. First, as noted above, the local lesbians and gay men are unorganized and appear to lack interest in social and political activism. The University of Southern Mississippi in Hattiesburg chartered its first lesbian, gay and bisexual group only four years ago. The social life of the young lesbians and gays focuses solely on one local bar. Drug and alcohol use and abuse is common. The Camp, which is a drug and alcohol free space, could be an alternative for the young lesbians and gay men, but only a few have shown any interest. The older lesbian and gay community is mostly closeted and quietly living bourgeois existences. The second, and related, reason that the local lesbian and gay community did not openly support the camp is the same as that of the Ovett citizens who support the camp: fear for their jobs, their homes, and their lives. Mississippi is a state where sodomy is still a felony and as long as there are no federal protections for lesbians and gay men, there will be no protection for lesbians and gays in Mississippi. Most lesbians and gays in Hattiesburg or Laurel are unwilling to risk their jobs, lives, etc., for the women of Camp Sister Spirit.

On the other hand, Camp Sister Spirit received much support, including physical labor and monetary contributions, from both individual lesbians and gay men throughout the United States and the world and from national organizations, including the NGLTF and the National Organization for Women. Some women traveling in the area visited and worked at the Camp for several days or even weeks. These women, however, were always free to leave if the threats and harassment became too real for them, so they were not taking the same risk as the caretakers.

Pattern #7: There Is a Legitimation of the Rituals of "Objective Scholarship," Despite Appearances of Disapproval

The events surrounding Camp Sister Spirit were widely addressed in the media. Most of the national coverage was balanced or even biased toward the women of Camp Sister Spirit. The local coverage of the dispute was somewhat more ambiguous. James Stewart, a doctoral student in USM's Speech Communication Department, did an analysis of the coverage in the *Hattiesburg American* of the dispute. He noted that the coverage was relatively balanced in terms of articles and letters to the editor, but that the editorials and opinion pieces clearly favored the Ovett opposition (Stewart, 1994, 5-10). However, with the removal of Ken Fortenberry as executive editor, the unsigned editorials leaned toward support for Camp Sister Spirit.

Stewart also examined the language used in reference to the retreat and the women in the paper's coverage. He noted that the paper tended to use value-laden terms when referring to the camp and the women. Stewart noted that in almost all the articles any term used to describe the camp was linked in the same sentence with the sexuality of the women. He also noted that over the course of the coverage, the term feminist appeared to be synonymous with lesbian (1994, 7).

The former executive editor of the *Hattiesburg American*, Ken Fortenberry, was clearly biased in his commentaries. In the March 6, 1994, Sunday edition, he described a visit to Ovett and the camp. The citizens of Ovett were described as hardworking, religious folk who did not seek any attention and publicity. The women were described as "defiant," and "angry." The community of Ovett was described as "little churches with old graveyards. Freshly tilled soil. Cows and more cows. Thick, green grass . . . some of the most beautiful land on earth." The camp, on the other hand, was "primitive at best. A couple of travel trailers here, junked couches there, and working women in T-shirts and blue jeans, one of them with a knife strapped to her side."

However, the coverage by the *American* was not the worst of the local coverage. The worst coverage was by the *Laurel Leader-Call*. It was particularly biased in its reporting and its publisher wrote an opinion piece early in the dispute that was a masterpiece of patriarchal rhetoric. In addition, the 10 December 1993 *Leader-Call* published a picture of a delivery truck outside the Camp with the heading:

> NO MEN ALLOWED–Residents of 'Camp Sister Spirit' stop a delivery truck at the entrance to the 'retreat' in the Ovett community. According to the group's newsletter, *Grapevine*, which avoids even mention of the male gender, men are not welcome, even men delivering building materials to the camp made up of a lesbian majority.

The Hensons never denied workers access to the camp.

While the local press coverage of the dispute in the *Hattiesburg American* was balanced in its articles and letters to the editors, by taking the side of Ovett in its editorials, commentary and op-ed pieces, it did serve to legitimate the opposition to the camp, both legal and illegal, despite the appearance of objectivity. The handling of this dispute by the *Leader-Call* was clearly intended to stir up opposition to the camp. On the other hand, the national media and press seemed to be somewhat more favorable to the Hensons and the women of the camp.

CONCLUSION

In the midst of the apparent spread of "hate" as a political strategy and the increasing use of violence by marginal groups, the dispute between Camp Sister Spirit and Ovett offers a timely example of cultural and political conflicts that seem to be playing themselves out with common or "ritualized" rhetoric and strategies. The dispute between the camp and Ovett was particularly ferocious because it was a conflict between two marginalized groups at opposite ends of the political and cultural spectrums. What was interesting, however, was that instead of being a private battle, this dispute quickly became public and almost immediately thereafter was transformed into a political and legal dispute utilizing the mainstream apparatus of the political and judicial systems. Ovett blamed the camp for making the dispute public, but both sides were willing to go public, and the evidence suggests that the camp went public with the dispute as a defensive measure and the Ovett opposition went public as a means of garnering support. It was also the Ovett opposition which immediately sought legal means to "force the women out of the community" (Marx, 10 December 1993).

Another interesting aspect of the dispute was the use of "blaming the victim" and scapegoating. Blaming the victim has long been a strategy used against women, but scapegoating, as noted by Sklar and Berlet, has increasingly become a strategy of the far right, including the religious right, against the poor, minorities, gays, and lesbians as well as heterosexual women. Abortion providers become murderers, welfare becomes a drain on public money, affirmative action becomes reverse discrimination, feminists become witches and lesbians, and lesbians become the seducers of wives and daughters. While Camp Sister Spirit did not engage in wholesale scapegoating, they, like the Ovett group, were concerned with the public representation of themselves. The women of Camp Sister Spirit saw themselves as being engaged in a civil rights struggle against intolerance, misogyny, and terrorism. The Ovett group saw itself as Christians whose beliefs and values were under attack by militant homosexuals. Somewhere in this struggle over representation, the real issue of whether Sister Spirit was free to establish a retreat on its own land was obscured. Even the press became involved in the question of representation and tended to highlight those aspects of the dispute over the legal claims. It was not until the nuisance suit came to trial that attention was focused on the property rights issue.

This conflict also showed how a hostile, homophobic atmosphere of public opinion can influence social and political action in a community. Certain groups, particularly young, white men, felt free to trespass on the land, to harass the women when they went into town, to threaten them with violence, and to loudly and publicly express anti-lesbian feelings. The publicly expressed attitude of the local sheriff that the women were paranoid and making up the threats did little to discourage such activity. One young man, whose sense was that it was acceptable to attack and kill gays, paid a high price. The hostility and fear surrounding the whole dispute also kept an already passive lesbian and gay community from actively supporting the women of Camp Sister Spirit. On the other hand, men and women from other parts of the country and the world came to Ovett, despite fear, to support women they believed to be in a struggle for civil rights. In some ways, this reflects the situation in Mississippi in the early 1960s when local whites who supported civil rights remained silent, also because of fear of ostracism and retaliation (Trillin, 1995).

One last point that was not made through use of the seven patterns involves the question of whether this is simply a dispute about lesbians and gays or if it is more than that. Analyzing this dispute as I did tended to downplay the extent to which this dispute is about women's rights as much as it is about lesbian rights or property rights. Camp Sister Spirit is intended to be a feminist educational retreat which serves all women and men who suffer economic disadvantage. It is about women working together to change the world that men have made and to remake it upon feminist values. In more practical terms, it is about women sharing food and clothes with those in need. It is about providing information to women who need the battered women's shelter or the sexual assault crisis center. It is also about women owning and controlling land in a world where women own less than 10% of the land. The men of Ovett understand this quite well and it is a strong part of their opposition to the camp. Wanda Henson recounted a story which shows that at least one other woman in Ovett understands this. According to Wanda, a large, strong woman at a farmer's market approached her and asked her name. When Wanda identified herself, the woman responded: "I thought so. This doesn't have anything to do with the fact that you're different." Wanda asked what she meant and the woman continued, "What's happening to you has to do with the fact that you are a woman. Look. I've been living in Ovett for 53 years and I'm a woman landowner, and I still have men trespassing on my property. Keep doing what you are doing because you are doing it for all of us" (Chesler, 1994, 63).

REFERENCES

Albert, Michael. 1992. "Conspiracy? . . . Not!" *Z Magazine*, January.

Alcoff, Linda. 1988. "Cultural Feminism versus Post-Structural Feminism: The Identity Crisis in Feminist Theory." *Signs: Journal of Women in Culture and Society*, 13 (No. 3):405-436.

Allen, John S. "The Homosexual Agenda and the Church: Silence Equals Consent," *The Baptist Record: Journal of the Mississippi Baptist Convention*, 6 January 1994.

Barrett, Paul. "Let Our Women Educate Sisters" *Laurel Leader-Call*, 28 December 1993.

Berlet, Chip. 1994 "The Right Rides High." *The Progressive*, June.

Braswell, Janet. 1993. "Ovett Residents Vow to Fight Sister Spirit Retreat," *Hattiesburg American*, 7 December 1993.

Braswell, Janet. "Mediators Removed from Ovett Dispute," *Hattiesburg American*, 19 March 1994.

Bundy, David. "Laurel Teen Jailed in Double Murder," *Hattiesburg American*, 13 October 1994.

Chesler, Phyllis. "Sister, Fear Has No Place Here." *On the Issues*, Fall 1994.

Christensen, Brent. "Camp Sister Spirit Hearing on Harassment Scheduled," *Hattiesburg American*, 30 June 1994.

Code, Lorraine. 1991. *What Can She Know? Feminist Theory and the Construction of Knowledge*. Ithaca: Cornell University Press.

Daly, Mary. 1978. *Gyn/Ecology: The Metaethics of Radial Feminism*. Boston: Beacon Press.

Daly, Mary. 1984. *Pure Lust Elemental Feminist Philosophy*. Boston: Beacon Press.

Faggart, Rob, "Lesbians Under Siege," *The Front Page*, 10 December 1993.

Fortenberry, Ken, "Commentary: A Clash of Values," *Hattiesburg American*, 6 March 1994.

Greene, Kate. 1994. Interviews and conversations with Wanda and Brenda Henson. January 8, by telephone; January 16; May 31; July 6; September 13, by telephone; and September 21.

_____. 1995. Interviews and conversations with Wanda Henson. May 21, by telephone.

Greene, Kate and Edward M. Wheat. 1995. "Camp Sister Spirit versus Ovett: Culture Wars in Mississippi," *Southeastern Political Review*, 23(2):315-332.

Hekman, Susan J. 1990. *Gender and Knowledge: Elements of a Postmodern Feminism*. Boston: Northeastern University Press.

Hendry, J.D. "Ovett Resident Says 'No, Thanks,' to Lesbian Retreat" *Hattiesburg American*, 28 November 1993.

Jaggar, Alison, M. 1983. *Feminist Politics and Human Nature*. Sussex: Harvester Press.

James, Eloria Newell. "Ovett Community Takes Dispute to National Audience," *Hattiesburg American*, 15 December 1993.

James, Eloria Newell. "Sister Spirit Foes Take Case Before County Officials," *Hattiesburg American*, 21 December 1993.

James, Eloria Newell. "Ovett Residents Protest Camp," *Hattiesburg American*, 4 January 1994.

James, Eloria Newell. "National Media Report on Ovett," *Hattiesburg American*, 4 January 1994.

James, Eloria Newell. "Residents Plan to Sue Ovett Camp," *Hattiesburg American*, 5 January 1994.

James, Eloria Newell. "County Stays Clear of Ovett Flap," *Hattiesburg American*, 5 January 1994.

James, Eloria Newell., "Woman Accused of Harassing Sister Spirit Foe," *Hattiesburg American*, 25 March 1994.

Lee, Anita. "Standing Firm," *Sun-Herald*, 31 July 1994.

Lorde, Audre. 1984. "An Open Letter to Mary Daly." *Sister Outsider*. Freedom: The Crossing Pen.

Marx, Hal. "Retreat Getting National Media Attention," *Laurel Leader-Call*, 10 December 1993.

Maute, Nikki Davis. "Women's Camp in Spotlight." *Hattiesburg American*, 11 December 1993.

Maute, Nikki Davis. "Ovett-area Activists Sue Reno," *Hattiesburg American*, 7 March 1994.

Maute, Nikki Davis. "Hearings on Ovett Feud Begin Today," *Hattiesburg American*, 6 July 1994.

Maute, Nikki Davis. "No Guarantees Made in Special Ovett Hearing," *Hattiesburg American*, 7 July 1994.

Maute, Nikki Davis. "Neighbors Say Feminists Deliberately Stirred Quarrel," *Hattiesburg American*, 18 May 1995.

Maute, Nikki Davis. "Neighbors Say Camp Sister Spirit Noisy," *Hattiesburg American*, 19 May 1995.

Maute, Nikki Davis. "Judge Considering Sister Spirit Case," *Hattiesburg American*, 23 May 1995.

McLaurin, Tarsha. "Reno Sends Mediators to Ovett," *Hattiesburg American*, 19 February 1994.

McLaurin, Tarsha. "Fund-raiser Fights Ovett Camp," *Hattiesburg American*, 6 March 1994.

"Mississippi Town Foiled By Lesbians' Plan for Women's Camp," *New York Times*, 11 January 1994 [missing data].

Powers, Shelley. "[Ocean] Springs Man to Discuss Gay Issue on Premiere of Rolanda Watts Show," *Mississippi Press*, 17 January 1994.

Remwolt, Lisa. "'Sister Spirit' Faces Opposition," *Sun-Herald*, 6 December 1993.

Remwolt, Lisa. "FBI Eyes Ovett Case," *Sun-Herald*, 15 January 1994.

Rubenstein, William B. *Lesbians, Gay Men and the Law*. New York: The New Press, 1993.

Sanford, Darrell. "Reno, *Hattiesburg American*, Lining Up Behind Gay, Liberal Agenda," *Hattiesburg American*, 6 March 1994.

Shows, Harvey. "Sister Spirit's Goal: Exalted 'Victimhood,'" *Hattiesburg American*, 26 December 1993.

Sklar, Holly. "The Snake Oil of Scapegoating." *Z Magazine*, May, 1995.

Slaton, Thad. "Sister Spirit Ruling Called a Victory; Appeal is Possible." *Hattiesburg American*, 6 July 1995.

Spelman, Elizabeth V. *Inessential Woman: Problems of Exclusion in Feminist Thought*. Boston: Beacon Press, 1988.

Stewart, James. "Coverage of the Sister Spirit Debate by the *Hattiesburg American*: A Case Study in Ethical Press Performance," unpublished manuscript, 1994.

Tisdall, Simon. "The Siege of Jones County." *The Guardian*, December 1993.

Trillin, Calvin. "State Secrets." *The New Yorker*, May 29, 1995.

Turque, Bill, Kelvin Gray, Ellen Ladowsky, and Peter Anin. "Mississippi Burning/Lesbians: Intolerance in a Small Town." *Newsweek*, 20 December 1993.

WHLT (CBS), *Oprah Winfrey Show*. 21 December 1993.

A Member of the Wedding?
Heterosexism and Family Ritual

Ramona Faith Oswald

SUMMARY. Heterosexism as an interpersonal dynamic at weddings was examined using feminist critical science. Data were collected from 45 gay, lesbian, bisexual, and transgender people who attended focus groups. Gay, lesbian, bisexual, and transgender participants described multiple interactions in which they were devalued or hidden while heterosexuality was elevated, as well as interactions in which they or another family member resisted heterosexism. Weddings were perceived to be difficult, and participation in them was questioned. As part of their critique of weddings, participants offered a vision of relationships that was based on commitment, rather than heterosexuality or material benefits. Results of this study were used to create a brochure and Website for educating heterosexual people planning weddings.

KEYWORDS. Ritual, lesbian, heterosexism, family of origin, weddings

Ramona Faith Oswald, PhD, is affiliated with the Department of Human and Community Development, 263 Bevier Hall, mc-180, 908 South Goodwin, Urbana, IL 61801 (E-mail: roswald@uiuc.edu).

This research was partially funded by a Doctoral Dissertation Special Grant from the University of Minnesota. A USDA Hatch Grant provided writing support.
Reprinted by permission of Sage Publications Ltd. from Ramona Faith Oswald, A Member of the Wedding? Heterosexism and Family Ritual, © *Journal of Social and Personal Relationships*, 17(3) 2000.

[Haworth co-indexing entry note]: "A Member of the Wedding? Heterosexism and Family Ritual." Oswald, Ramona Faith. Co-published simultaneously in *Journal of Lesbian Studies* (Harrington Park Press, an imprint of The Haworth Press, Inc.) Vol. 7, No. 2, 2003, pp. 107-131; and: *Lesbian Rites: Symbolic Acts and the Power of Community* (ed: Ramona Faith Oswald) Harrington Park Press, an imprint of The Haworth Press, Inc., 2003, pp. 107-131.

Proud mothers and tearful fathers. Beaming brides, nervous grooms, and grandparents offering advice. Poses and flashbulbs and itchy clothes. Petty arguments behind closed doors. Children abuzz with too much cake and excitement. Boisterous friends kidding each other about whom will be next. Although perhaps the most normative of rituals, weddings are not neutral. Rituals are significant in part because they link private and public meanings, and demonstrate an acceptance and/or rejection of social convention (Roberts, 1988). Our society privileges heterosexual marriage, and thus weddings also link the personal decision to marry with an institutional heterosexual privilege carrying profound social, legal, financial, and religious benefits. These benefits are not currently available to gay, lesbian, bisexual, and transgender (GLBT) people. In addition, within current public discourse and policy, privilege linked to the union of one man and one woman is bolstered by defining GLBT people as a threat to family life based in heterosexual marriage (e.g., Federal Defense of Marriage Act, 1996). Thus, weddings not only celebrate heterosexuality, they also symbolize the multiple social benefits surrounding marriage that are denied, GLBT people. Weddings, therefore, offer a unique opportunity to examine ways in which power relations between heterosexual and GLBT people may be reproduced. The purpose of this study is to examine whether, and how, GLBT family members perceive heterosexism at family weddings.

Weddings are not, however, theorized to be simplistically scripted events that are or are not heterosexist. Like all rituals, proper weddings are proscribed by social authority (Parkin, 1992). Given that family members are front-stage (Goffman, 1959) during weddings, they are likely to construct an image of themselves that is consistent with social proscriptions (Cheal, 1988) even if that image belies their non-ritual way of interacting. Because ritual is a kind of social performance (Goffman, 1959), the discovery of heterosexism at weddings should not be surprising, even when it is experienced by GLBT people who are out and relatively accepted in everyday life. In addition, any analysis of weddings should allow for the possibility that proper enactment is subverted as individuals pursue their own meanings and desires in social interaction with others (Parkin, 1992). This potential co-existence of multiple and competing realities brings out Baumann's (1992) claim that rituals implicate otherness; they are always constructed with reference to an outside group. Thus, while many aspects of ritual can be understood by looking only at the in-group experience, our knowledge will be deepened, and even challenged, when we look at how that ritual is experienced and/or perceived by members of the out-group who affect, and are affected by, the ritual. In the case of weddings, GLBT people do constitute an out-group in relation to heterosexuals, and their experience potentially corrects and expands current knowledge about weddings, about family, and about the consequences social inequality may have for personal relationships.

The few interpretive studies of heterosexual weddings and related rituals that have been published have not questioned the heterosexist social context in which family relations are negotiated. For example, Braithwaite and Baxter (1995) interviewed husbands and wives about their vow-renewal ceremonies. Participants emphasized the importance of having their renewals be like conventional weddings, but did not acknowledge the existence of any GLBT family members, or the impact that their ritual choice might have had on others. While Braithwaite and Baxter (1995) examined how wives and husbands use vow renewal to maintain their relationships, most other wedding scholars have analyzed the social construction of gender. Cheal (1988) observed bridal showers and argued that they are sites of female solidarity where women affirm the ties that they will need in order to survive sexist marriages. Currie (1993) interviewed brides about their wedding planning processes and found that they opted for traditional symbolism and behavior that subordinated them to their husbands. Brides defined their choice as a matter of personal preference rather than adherence to tradition. Braithwaite (1995) participated in co-ed wedding showers and analyzed the ways in which women, being the ritual experts, embarrassed men into complying with ritual practices. These existing studies demonstrate the intercom (Roberts, 1988) by which social interaction during ritual aligns individual behavior and desires with social norms that promote conventional gender and heterosexual relationships. This study will add to existing knowledge an understanding of what happens within personal relationships when presumptions of universal heterosexuality are interrupted.

METHODOLOGY

Feminist critical science guided this investigation. Demo and Allen (1996) argued that the family field needs more research on gay and lesbian people from a variety of paradigms, including critical science. The goal of feminist critical science research is to promote social justice by using empirical research to challenge beliefs and practices that exclude non-hegemonic experience and knowledge (Lather, 1991). This goal requires the development of a standpoint (Comstock, 1982).

Reflexive practice, the process by which relationships between self, social location, and knowledge are analyzed, aids in the development of standpoint (Lather, 1991). Having a standpoint is a first step towards challenging injustice; it enables people to see the ways in which hegemonic discourse privileges some perspectives while obscuring others, and it links this process to ongoing material inequalities in society (Comstock, 1982). My own evolving critical consciousness is the base from which this project developed. During two very intense years, I attended family weddings, had co-workers who got married, and my partner and I had a commitment ceremony. I initially thought about the various exclusions that I experienced as products of specific interpersonal relationships. It was only after talking with many other GLBT people that I was able to think about heterosexism and weddings as a shared rather than idiosyncratic experience. I began to identify myself as a member of a marginalized group rather than someone who just had an alternative lifestyle and a difficult family.

Despite my developing standpoint, I was challenged throughout this project to rethink the constructed "myth of us" (Harraway, 1990, p. 197): GLBT people are not necessarily alike. I have learned to take seriously the importance of religion in people's lives, the pull of family loyalty, and the desire of many to participate in mainstream culture so that I can engage in "open and flexible theory building, grounded in a body of empirical work ceaselessly confronted with, and respectful of, the experiences of people in their daily lives" (Lather, 1991, p. 54).

Thus, when I sought to use Comstock's (1982) method for critical research, I could not follow it exactly. He began with the investigator working with an established group, and implied that the researcher is an outsider to the group who tries to understand insider meanings. Because I am an insider, and GLBT group membership is not organized in a formal way around weddings, I instead conceptualized this research more loosely as a community project. Participants were recruited through community venues and I presented myself as a lesbian who wanted to know what other GLBT people had experienced at weddings. Flyers, newspaper and Internet postings, and word of mouth recruiting were all used to locate participants.

Participants

Recruiting took place within Minneapolis-St. Paul, Minnesota, a place in which GLBT people are highly visible and relatively accepted. Response was rapid–most participants were recruited within two weeks. Forty-five adult GLBT people who had attended at least one heterosexual family wedding participated. They ranged in age from eighteen to seventy-one years. Forty-two participants attended one of nine focus groups, and two gay male participants attended two focus groups because they felt that they had more to say.

Twenty-six participants identified as female, fifteen as male, and four as something other than male or female (I will refer to them as transgender). Twenty-four women identified as lesbian, fourteen men identified as gay, and two women and one man identified as bisexual. One transgender participant claimed a bisexual identity, while the other three self-identified as queer, femme, or oriented to drag culture.

I had originally planned to recruit only gay male and lesbian woman participants. However, it quickly became clear to me that doing so would unnecessarily alienate members of the community who identified themselves as other than gay or lesbian, male or female. Rust (1992, 1993) argued that social scientists typically ignore bisexuality, or conceptualize it as homosexuality. When recruiting for this study, I tried to be inclusive of the range of non-heterosexual identities. I use the acronym GLBT because insiders considered it the inclusive and correct identifier for this community.

Thirty-three participants were white with primarily northern and central European ancestry, and twelve participants were people of color with African, Hispanic, Native, and Caribbean ancestry. An attempt was made to recruit people of color for the first six groups. When this largely failed, three groups were added that specifically welcomed people of color. This was successful when I personally invited participation, and relied upon personal contacts that vouched for my trustworthiness.

Seventeen participants grew up in Catholic families, but only seven were currently practicing. Nineteen participants claimed no religious identity, eleven belonged to a Christian denomination, six were Jewish, and five practiced Wicca (numbers do not add up to forty-five as people could claim more than one religion).

Thirty-one participants described themselves as middle class, seven as poor, and three as working class. The remaining three refused to answer the question. Twenty-three participants worked in human services, seven were students, five did clerical work, three were political activists, and three did not answer the question (not the same three that refused to indicate class). There was also an engineer, an accountant, a mechanic, and a retired dress designer.

In addition to providing demographic information, participants rated the degree to which they were out to themselves as GLBT ($M = 5.7$), and the degree to which they were out to their families ($M = 5.0$), on a scale of one to six. The mean scores suggest that participants were committed to living openly as GLBT, and at least one other person in their family of origin was aware of their sexual orientation. It is important to realize in the analysis presented below that at every wedding some (or all) family members were aware of the GLBT person's sexual orientation.

Focus Group Interviews

Comstock's (1982) second step is for the researcher to work with the group to construct intersubjective agreement about the experience of oppression. Participants are encouraged to talk not only about their experiences, but also about what those experiences mean, and why they participated in the way that they did. This is not to say that group members have to have identical experiences or interpretations, but rather they should come to some understanding that what they have experienced is linked to power relations that also affect other group members. To facilitate this, it is important to create what Habermas referred to as an ideal speech situation (in Rediger, 1996) in which participants are not afraid to speak openly. For this reason, interviews were held in locations considered friendly and familiar. They lasted approximately two hours and thirty minutes. I served pizza as a way to facilitate group bonding before the interview started.

During the interviews, participants were asked about (a) their general opinion of heterosexual weddings; (b) their experiences at the last wedding they attended; (c) how their experiences were shaped by gender, culture, class, age, race, and religion; (d) why they chose to attend; (e) how they knew that their experiences were real (i.e., what criteria they used in order to validate their experience given that they were interacting with people and symbols who were often invalidating); (f) what they would like to have been different; and (g) how they would like this research to be used. These open-ended questions were intended to generate data about weddings without imposing researcher preconceptions.

Patricia Nelson, my African-American lesbian research assistant, and I alternated responsibility for facilitation and recording. As facilitators we took a fluid approach, covering all topics but following the group lead when deciding when to ask each question. The interviews generally proceeded as Krueger (1994) suggested, starting with general, moving to specific, and ending with application and closure. As recorders we were silent and tried to sit outside the group (although in two locations this was not possible) so that everyone sitting at the table would be an active participant.

I intentionally recruited a qualified assistant who was of a different race from myself (I am white) with the intent of constructing a research environment in which differences were noticed and accepted at both the visual and verbal level of experience (it turned out that we also differed by age and class). Participants were told that we were interested in hearing about their lives and that we expected people to have differences and disagreements. They were encouraged to ask questions of each other, and of us. There was evidence of intersubjective agreement such as when participants nodded, agreed, reproduced, and expanded upon each other's stories. At the same time, each interview also had multiple instances where participants disagreed with each other or pointed out how their experience was different from someone else's. In the below analysis, I integrate a range of perspectives and experiences.

Immediately after each interview, I sent each participant a thank you card. A week later, I tried to contact all participants for a check-in. I asked the 31 participants who I reached what they thought about their experience, if they had anything to add about weddings, and if there was anything I could do for them related to this project. Responses indicated that the experience was positive and that people wanted to receive any materials that were developed.

Data Analysis

Because critical science attends to the language of participants and the group dynamics out of which data is constructed (Comstock, 1982), interviews were audio-recorded, and then transcribed verbatim. Transcription produced approximately 300 single spaced pages of data. Because transcripts were completed over the course of several months, I analyzed them in the order in which they were completed. After using open and axial coding procedures (Strauss & Corbin, 1991) with data from focus groups one, two, and four, the performance and resistance of heterosexism emerged as a core category to which other categories were linked. Core categories are threads that pull together and explain other categories (Strauss & Corbin, 1991). Although we never directly asked about heterosexism, without it, none of the data made sense. Heterosexism was the thread that pulled together and explained the myriad of interactions, meanings, and motives that participants expressed. The remaining six transcripts were then selectively coded (Strauss & Corbin, 1991) for data regarding the enactment of, and resistance to, heterosexism. By analyzing both heterosexism and anti-heterosexism I was able to integrate a range of experience within one theoretical frame, and avoid presenting heterosexism as all encompassing. In addition, my constant comparative selective coding process (Strauss & Corbin, 1991) was such that I continually moved back and forth between transcripts and analysis looking for data that would qualify or contradict my emerging theory.

Validity

Ensuring that the researcher has captured participant realities is the next step in Comstock's (1982) method. Lather (1991) calls this working to obtain the yes-of-course response from participants. Toward this end, a draft of this manuscript was mailed to each participant and honest comments were requested. Comments were offered over the phone or in person, and were positive. In addition, two participants returned the manuscript filled with editorial comments.

Critical science research has catalytic validity (Lather, 1991) when it results in social change. Praxis refers to the process of moving between research and social change. Comstock's (1982) conception of praxis involves the researcher working with the group over time to put their knowledge into action. However, he assumes that the researcher is working with an established group that is committed to social action. This assumption did not fit the design of this study (see above). In addition, given the constraints of graduate school, it was not realistic for me to pursue an ongoing social action relationship with participants (Rettig, Tam, & Yellowthunder, 1995). My compromise was to ask how they would like the results of this study to be used. Participants overwhelmingly wanted their family members (and other heterosexual people) to access expert information about how to include them in family events. They did not, however, want to be the experts. At their request, I used the results presented here to create an educational brochure and matching Website (www.staff.uiuc.edu/~roswald) targeting heterosexual people who are planning weddings. Both include practical advice about how to be inclusive, offer resources, and encourage readers to think about the impact of heterosexism on them and their GLBT loved ones. The Website includes a guest book where visitors can post their own experiences at weddings. The brochure has been distributed in three different states, and the Website has received over 800 hits since its creation. Participants have been instrumental in the distribution of brochures despite their lack of involvement in creating the actual copy. Although the brochure/Website project does not strictly adhere to Comstock's (1982) interpretation of praxis, I believe it is true to the spirit of critical science.

Although praxis in this study is limited, there is evidence that participation led to varying degrees of critical consciousness. Before attending a focus group, most participants in this study had thought about weddings in terms of their personal experience as well as political implications. Some had engaged in political discussions. However, few had discussed their experiences with other GLBT people in any depth, and none had openly discussed their feelings and experiences with heterosexual family members. I believe that the research design used led participants to think more deeply about how their lives are and are not shaped by heterosexism, and what they might do about it. In their closing statements, and in follow up comments, many participants indicated that they had come to be more reflexive than reactive about weddings. Their "ideologically frozen conceptions the actual and the possible" (Comstock, 1982, p. 371) had thawed into a sense that they had choices about how to participate, and had clarified their own values about marriage in relation to dominant discourse.

RESULTS AND DISCUSSION

Heterosexism was central to the experience of GLBT people at family weddings. It contributed to a sense that weddings were rife with social meanings and practices that devalued GLBT people. A sense of emptiness and unfairness at weddings was pervasive, and led participants to question, and even avoid, participation in these family rituals. Exceptions to this main narrative are integrated into the analysis presented below.

Doing Heterosexism

Heterosexism in this study was a dynamic whereby heterosexuality was elevated while GLBT identities and relationships were hidden or devalued. Thus, heterosexism was not a property of individuals, nor was it merely a contextual factor. Like gender in Walker (1996; see also West and Zimmerman, 1987), heterosexism emerged from social interaction that linked ideology with behavior. Given that heterosexism is also a macro-level phenomenon, this finding supports symbolic interactionist, feminist, and ritual theory assumptions that social and cultural meanings and practices are negotiated within interpersonal interaction (Cheal, 1988; LaRossa & Reitzes, 1993; Osmond & Thorne, 1993).

Behavior is neutral with regards to meaning; action is meaningful or purposeful behavior that is shaped by conditions not necessarily under the control, or in the awareness, of the actor (Comstock, 1982). Whether due to ignorance, ambivalence, or meanness, all of the heterosexism reported by participants was *perceived* to be action rather than behavior. Given the design of this study, there is no way to determine what those they interacted with were intending or perceiving.

What follows is an account of how heterosexism was performed and resisted from the onset to the conclusion of the wedding ritual. Because critical science accounts should reflect the language of participants (Comstock, 1982), I make extensive use of quotes. All participants have been given pseudonyms.

Invitations. Wedding invitations are typically extended to both partners in a heterosexual couple or, if the heterosexual person is single, to that person and a guest. When invitations were sent to GLBT family members, and either allowed for a guest or invited a partner, then these invitations were small but profound gestures that symbolized the GLBT person's inclusion in their family of origin, and the sender was perceived as resisting heterosexism. When invitations were not sent to GLBT family members, or were sent with conditions that pressured the GLBT person to hide or change, then the act of inviting was perceived as doing heterosexism.

Most participants were invited to family weddings. Several, however, were not. Gloria Ramierez, was not invited to her aunt's wedding "because they're really prejudiced . . . they won't talk to me because I'm bisexual." Gloria attended the wedding anyway "because it was this big family event and I would be the only person not there." Her aunt then told her not to attend the reception. Gloria conceded the struggle and went home.

GLBT people who were in long-term relationships recalled wedding invitations where their partners were not invited. For example, Lucy Gibbons was invited to a wedding where the bride called and "specifically asked me to not bring Karen to the wedding . . . it was appalling to me . . . she had this fear that I was going to bring Karen and embarrass her." Karen did not attend the wedding because she was not welcome, and Lucy attended as if she were single; they did not resist.

Some relatives resisted heterosexism by allowing or encouraging their GLBT family members to bring a date to the wedding. GLBT family members felt tremendously affirmed when this happened. For example, Aaron Loeffler's cousin "called and said 'you know what, we want to make sure that you bring somebody and that be whomever you want, that person is welcome.'" Aaron went on to say that he had:

> been to weddings where [his date or partner] isn't included, and they know that I'm gay, and they specifically leave off the 'and guest' part even though all the rest of my friends or family have 'and guest' listed on theirs . . . when people include 'and guest' it's definitely an ally move. [the group agrees]

When their partners were invited, several GLBT family members were compelled to attend the wedding just to reciprocate the support shown to them by the sender. Barbara Greene and her partner attended a wedding together after they had broken up just because both their names were on the invitation. Having her relationship validated on an invitation by family members was so important that Debbie Miller, who has attended more than 25 family weddings, "saved every envelope that says 'Debbie Miller and guest.'"

Clothing. GLBT family members who attended weddings agonized over what to wear. Dressing up is expected at weddings because it symbolizes both the importance of the event, and the demarcation of ritual from everyday life. GLBT participants did not challenge the belief that wedding guests should wear special clothes, but they did seek to break rules about what those special clothes could be. Participants struggled with how to "feel comfortable for who I am, and yet not make other people uncomfortable" (Terry Novitski).

What one wears symbolizes who one is; clothing signifies identity. In order to maintain the heterosexual meaning within weddings, participants need to appear heterosexual, which means that they need to look conventionally male and female. Participants felt intense pressure to comply with this symbolism. Several lesbians who conformed to the rules of dress described their attire as "being in drag" because it meant that they physically represented exaggerated notions of helpless and petite femininity that were incongruent with their "zaftig" bodies and lesbian or bisexual identities. Nathan Lowry was told by his parents not to wear a festive tie because it "looked too trendy [meaning gay]." A male-to-female transgender guest wore flowing pants to one family wedding and has since been banned from attending any others: "They're calling it a dress now, but it wasn't" (Jess Avery).

Breaking gendered dress codes limits heterosexual power by presenting other options for identities and relationships. It was difficult, however, for lesbians to break gender rules and not play into stereotypes that they want to look or act like heterosexual men. For example, Debbie Miller intended to wear a tuxedo in her sister's wedding but changed into a dress at the last minute because all fourteen groomsmen were wearing her chosen outfit: "It was this huge crisis for me, and my sister was very homophobic. . . . I didn't have the gall to wear the tuxedo because I didn't want to look like them." Within the GLBT community, Debbie's tuxedo would perhaps have been seen as "lesbian" rather than "male." The contextual nature of identity implied here suggests that the struggle to dress appropriately is the struggle to translate meaning from a supportive social context to one in which there is no foundation on which who one is can be expressed or understood.

At weddings where at least some family members were openly supportive of their GLBT relatives, lesbians felt more permission to dress as they wished. For some that meant wearing "an awesome dress" (Laura Bryce), and for others it meant wearing pants. Kaitlin Owens felt permission to challenge her sister's choice of a bridesmaid's dress because she was out to her: "My sister would hold up some ridiculous dress and say, 'Oh I think you should try this on.' But then I would suggest some equally hideous dresses for her. So we compromised." Several lesbians described the process by which they decided to wear comfortable clothes. For example, it took Rosa Mancini "four weddings to figure out that I could wear a vest, slacks, and loafers."

The Wedding Party. Being asked to participate in the wedding party is an act of inclusion. GLBT family members who were bridesmaids and groomsmen participated in the ritual construction of family and friend support for the couple getting married. This was, however, a mixed blessing. As bridesmaids paired up with groomsmen, and vice versa, GLBT family members were expected to symbolize heterosexuality during the wedding while hiding their GLBT identities and same-sex relationships. For example, Beth Stein was a bridesmaid, and her partner was the Matron of Honor, at a wedding where the bride and groom tried to keep their relationship submerged from view. Beth and her partner resisted invisibility by coming out as a couple:

> The Matron of Honor walks in with the Best Man, and so who was I supposed to walk with? . . . I ended up being paired with this kind of football player, tall, straight guy who drank lots of beer . . . and the bride and groom did not take the time to say who I was. You know, there would be these social things like parties and little things and they would go, okay, 'This is so and so and his wife blah blah,' 'and this is so and so his wife, blah blah,' 'and this is Beth . . .' They wouldn't say what our relationship was. And it was like, after having a commitment ceremony and being with my partner for 25 years I thought, 'Oh, did you forget already that *we're* married?' [she laughs]. And this kept happening, so my partner continued bringing up exactly who we were. So we're rehearsing and I'm supposed to be going in with this football player, and he goes, 'So! So! How do you know the bride or the groom?' And I just said, 'Well, I'm a [she sighs], her sister is my partner.' And he goes, 'OH! What business?' [the group laughs]. And I said, "We're lesbians." And he went, 'Ooooh.'

God Talk. Religion permeated the weddings described in this study. It served to promote heterosexuality as a religious imperative, and denigrate homosexuality. This denigration was felt by participants who listened to "the religious figure standing in front of however many people saying 'the Lord this, the Lord that,' you know, 'your vows are recognized by the Lord.' When I'm sitting there it feels like the priest or minister is saying 'you don't belong here because you're queer'" (Jason Royball).

GLBT family members listened to the religiously based sexist and procreative content of weddings that they attended, and quietly disagreed. During the focus group interview, participants voiced their concerns. Dave Knaebel said:

> Before I came out, I'd go to a wedding and hear the vows and be all emotional and happy, and nowadays I hear, 'You must obey your husband' and 'you must be fruitful and multiply' and 'bear children,' and suddenly the wedding becomes very uncomfortable.

Hannah Sadler heard Catholic vows that "allude to the man being dominant, 'I'm going to be your protector, ruler, Promise Keeper, white knight' . . . and that incites me . . . and it sort of scares me that people say these things and don't question them." GLBT relationships are typically organized by an ethic of equality, not domination (Kurdek, 1993), and marriage is not a cultural prerequisite for GLBT parenthood. The procreative and sexist imperative heard by GLBT participants was not only offensive, it didn't mesh with their cultural expectations.

Hearing the validation that heterosexual couples automatically receive for conforming to religious expectations exacerbated already hard feelings about being invisible and/or invalidated. For example, Susan Peterson is a practicing Christian, and her brother is serving a life sentence for murdering his girlfriend. Susan attended his wedding in prison and was "so taken with the fact that . . . everybody was okay with this wedding . . . everyone was so supportive and 'God this' and 'God that' and I thought, you know, I couldn't even bring a woman into this family and have her be welcomed, and yet my brother's wedding is accepted and welcomed and he's a *murderer*."

In addition to listening, some GLBT family members were lay readers in the ceremony. They voiced the very ideas that excluded them. For example, at her brother's wedding, Lynn Regan read a passage from the Bible about God blessing all married couples. Lynn's family is fundamentalist Christian. She considered resisting by saying "all couples" rather than "all married couples," but couldn't find the nerve. Kaitlin Owens, who is comfortably out within her family of origin, and whose family attends a more liberal church, was able to negotiate the reading with her sister. Kaitlin read "my love is like a leaping stag" from the Songs of Solomon, rather than a passage inferring that God ordains only heterosexual couples.

Family Portraits. Wedding portraits document who is considered a family member and who is not. They are artifacts shown to others, and thus they incorporate beliefs about how a family should be represented publicly. If GLBT family members (or their partners) are included in pictures, then their membership is solidified. Family photographs presented a situation in which GLBT guests questioned whether they and/or their partner would be included. For example, Beth Stein and her partner attended a Christian wedding in the bride's rural hometown. Beth and her family did not know how safe it was for them to be openly Jewish. When it was time for family photographs, the photographer did not understand that Beth and Sarah were a couple and kept trying to separate them when all other couples were positioned together. Finally the bride yelled, "They're together!" Beth said that:

> We felt confused and surrounded . . . and my family of origin was silent, my brother [the groom] didn't say a word. It was the bride who decided to say something, and part of it was that we were on her turf, but, there's

> this blending stuff about being Jewish, of trying not to make waves, but also there's this stuff about speaking out against oppression, and here was a place where my family chose to blend in, they could have stood up for me and they didn't. I felt very let down.

Other participants were excluded from photographs; their existence as family members erased in one quick flash. Lori Milford was in the back of the room at her brother's wedding when she noticed that the family photographs had been taken without her:

> And I thought, did the photographer not know that there was also a sister? All the questions that suddenly came through my mind, and yet my emotions were so close to the surface that I couldn't ask, I felt too vulnerable to ask, 'Was I supposed to be in this picture and if so can we take it again?'. . . nobody noticed, my brother never said 'Wait a minute, my sister should be here.'

Believing that they would be excluded led some participants to resist by avoiding the situation. Karen Johnson and her partner:

> ducked out of my brother's wedding after the cake thing so as to avoid the family pictures. Because I know what would have happened. She would not have been recognized as family in those orchestrated pictures, and that would have just killed me . . . we ditched, basically. . . . At that point I'd rather that my family deal with my unexplained absence of me in the photos than me having to live with the absence of my partner in them.

Catch the Bouquet and Garter. Participants understood catching the bouquet to be a time when unmarried females unite around the possibility of heterosexual marriage for all women, and compete with each other to be next. Where the bouquet ritual symbolized the importance of marriage for women, the garter ritual was understood to symbolize male bonding over the sexual domination of women within marriage. The values underlying these rituals were in conflict with the values held by GLBT family members. Participants described the bouquet ritual as silly, but were "repulsed by the whole idea of degrading this woman who just got married" (Dave Knaebel). "The garter is not fun, it's angering. It's like, you're marrying her so now you're going to show the other men her leg? . . . This brings us right back to the ownership of women. 'What's important in a wedding?' 'Oh yes, the way the bride's leg looks.' Yuk" (Laura Bryce).

A few single lesbians in this study were able to participate jokingly in the bouquet ritual: "Every once in a while I'll get in there and try to catch the bouquet, which is like a brilliant joke amongst all my friends" (Hilary Smith). Other GLBT family members participated half-heartedly in whichever gender ritual they felt pressured to embrace. Joseph Montero "just stood there and tried to look like I was interested in the garter, but it was hard for me." Many GLBT family members, single or coupled, avoided the garter and bouquet by getting refills on their drinks, taking pictures, or making some other socially appropriate excuse. Several sighed with relief when brides and grooms chose not to pursue these rituals: "It was really nice for me to not have to face that [and pretend] that I'm out there trying to catch the flowers" (Ann Heller).

During the bouquet and garter rituals, GLBT guests (even those who were 'out' and in committed relationships) perceived heterosexual guests as treating them as if they were single women and men who desired heterosexual marriage: "I think the bouquet is the worst part of the wedding for me. Because, like even when I was there with my partner, people were like, 'Get up there, you're single!' And I'd be like, 'fuck you!' . . . I just find it so frustrating and so humiliating" (Terry Novitski).

Pharr (1988) theorized that gay men are equated with women as a way to negatively sanction homosexuality, and in this study gay men found themselves "shunted into a female role" (Kyle Monroe) during the bouquet ritual. Nathan Lowry:

> was sitting down with all my friends and all the girls got up to catch the bouquet. And one of my male friends hits me and says, like, 'Why aren't you going up there?' Which at first I thought was really cool, but then I realized that he was kidding, and then, I'm like, 'yeah, whatever, dork' [the group laughs]. Yeah, no kidding . . . it was just so awkward, because with whom am I supposed to associate? Especially since some of my friends are associating me with the girls who are going up there.

Dancing. GLBT family members consciously decided whether or not to dance during the reception. Dancing at weddings was described as a performance governed by the following heterosexist rules: Men and women are expected to dance together, and "women can dance together, maybe not slow dance, but . . . two men who dance together are out to get laughs, you know. My family would joke, 'Oh the groom is going to dance with the best man, ha ha ha,' and it was meant to be hilarious. It was meant to be ridiculed . . . because 'just look what they're suggesting'" (Dave Knaebel).

Faced with these perceived rules, many participants chose not to dance. Some explained their decision as a product of internalized homophobia: "I feel threatened by the possibility of going up there, it's that homophobia inside of me pushing out going, 'Oh there's no way I can pull my lover on the dance floor'" (Aaron Loeffler). Other participants felt coerced by homophobia within the ritual, rather than within themselves: "We were together, people saw us together, but somehow . . . we had pushed every barrier, but that was one we couldn't break through" (Karen MacDonald).

The pressure to dance in heterosexual pairings was deeply felt. For example, against her wishes Joan Prutsman felt expected to, and did, dance with a groomsman at her mother's wedding, and Barbara Greene felt obliged to dance with her estranged father, who led despite her insistence that she didn't want to follow. At several weddings, the pressure to dance heterosexually was overlaid with expectations of heterosexual matchmaking: Dave Knaebel went to a wedding alone (because his partner was specifically not invited) and during the reception, where:

> a heterosexual aura filled the room, um, suddenly everyone was trying to set me up [with a woman] . . . they'd ask me questions and just try to be really heavy matchmakers . . . and I wasn't comfortable . . . but I submitted to the pressures to a certain extent. I danced with her.

Carl Schultz left his brother's reception because his relatives kept saying, "Oh don't you want to dance with that woman or that girl?"

Some participants subverted this pressure by seeking out "safe" heterosexual dancing partners such as cousins or siblings. Others used polite excuses to avoid the situation: "slow song, bathroom break . . . slow dance, time to leave again" (Dave Knaebel). The dollar dance, a staple in working class weddings where guests pay a dollar to dance with the bride or groom, provided an opportunity for GLBT guests to break the perceived heterosexual-pairing rule. Several participants described how they were the only one of their sex in line to dance with the bride or groom. For example, Jason Royball "stands in the line for the groom . . . it's always a joke, but it's never a joke for me . . . because I don't make it a two second dance–they're dancing with me. I get my dollar's worth!" On the other hand, several participants described how they wanted to dance with the bride or groom but "didn't feel free to do it" and sat out (Terry Novitski).

A few lesbian couples danced together non-sexually after negotiating the issue: At her father's wedding in rural New England, Laura Bryce's partner did not want to dance as a couple because "some redneck will come and shoot us." Laura replied, "Look, if they're here they're here for my father's wedding–they're not going to turn around and shoot his daughter on the way out.

Maybe the next day [she laughs], but not on the way out! Once we got past that we danced, but the fear was pretty real."

When same-sex couples overtly resisted the perceived rules and danced together as lovers, they had a profound impact on other GLBT guests. Joseph Montero watched two men slow dance and "wanted that to be me! . . . I was like, 'Oh my gosh! Look at that, look at those guys!' . . . It just felt so different to see two guys do it . . . it was pretty incredible." Beth Stein and her partner were the only lesbian couple dancing:

> and we were dancing slow songs and fast songs and we were just out there, we had a great time . . . and at the end of the reception the bride's mom came out to everyone as a lesbian! She was just sobbing, the bride hadn't known, it was incredibly moving, it was this gift . . . the bride's mother's partner was there as 'the roommate' and it's like, us being out dancing at this wedding was a catalyst for someone to come out and for a family to get closer.

Silencing. Rituals usually include some proscription against talk that would challenge or contradict the symbols being enacted (Roberts, 1988). GLBT guests in this study often felt obliged to not say anything about their personal lives even when they observed heterosexual guests doing so. For example, Kyle Monroe heard people talking:

> about what was new in their love lives, their marriages, whatever, and all of a sudden when they got to me it was 'well, um.' Even though they knew I had just moved in with my boyfriend. 'So are you going back to school? What's your favorite color?' [the group laughs].

Heterosexual guests were not perceived as telling GLBT family members to remain silent. Rather, participants described a sense of feeling coerced by the ritual, of "pretending to be straight even though everyone there knew I was gay, but I was still acting straight because I *couldn't be* gay [in that setting]" (Nathan Lowry).

Like all other dynamics described in this paper, silencing was resisted. A few GLBT guests did try to talk about themselves even though they felt ignored or discounted for doing do. For example, Amber Lawrence mentioned happily that she "had a new lover!" but noticed people glazing over and changing the subject. Also, there were heterosexual guests who went out of their way to talk openly with their GLBT relatives. Carl Schultz's sister, for example, kept checking in with him to see if he was doing okay. Stories of guests who tried to include them, even if their attempts appeared awkward, were shared.

For example, Lynn Regan was approached by a woman who patted her arm and asked very sincerely, "Did you have to come out like Ellen [DeGeneres]?" [the group laughs].

Pressure to Marry. At the same time that GLBT family members were expected to keep their lives quiet, they were sometimes asked "when are you going to get married?" The question was perceived as a kind of "double-whammy" that increased feelings of discomfort. For example, Anthony Watson was physically ill in his car after attending a wedding where he hid being gay. At that wedding, everyone had been asking, "Oh when's Anthony getting married?" He wondered:

> How do I tell these people that there's no damn way I'm getting married in the traditional sense of having a big Italian wedding, you know?! It's just a weird struggle inside of you when you're sitting there and all the people are wondering, 'where's your girlfriend?' . . . It's a very uncomfortable feeling.

Some participants were asked when they would marry even by people who knew they were GLBT. The question is perhaps asked of anyone at a wedding who is not heterosexually married, and is perhaps offensive to anyone who feels that heterosexual marriage should be a choice rather than an obligation. It had an additional meaning for GLBT guests, however, in light of the fact that same-sex marriage is illegal, and because it put them in the position of wondering whether or not it is safe to come out to the person asking. GLBT family members not faced with this question were those who felt that their GLBT identities and same-sex partners were more or less accepted within their extended families of origin.

The Meaning of Weddings

In order to more fully understand the experiences of GLBT people, we need to know what meaning they attach to that experience (Comstock, 1982). Brief discussion of meaning differences between GLBT and heterosexual family members was offered in the above analysis when it related to specific constructs being explored. I now explore the more over-arching meanings about weddings that were implied or described by participants.

Hollow rituals are experienced when the symbols constructed are not congruent with the symbols desired, and/or when they are performed out of obligation rather than sincerity (Roberts, 1988). In this study, participants used the term hollow repeatedly to suggest that weddings exclude them, and they felt that conventionally scripted weddings were especially alienating. Many GLBT family members appreciated the "promise and the hope at weddings" and the sense that marriage was an incredible "act of faith between two people" (Thomas Kincaid). However, "there were also feelings of jealousy . . . because I'm *never* going to be able to share that experience with my family in the way that my brother did" (Ann Heller).

Participants also felt that weddings were overly materialistic, that family members tended to focus on gifts and money more than the commitment being made. For example, Thomas Kincaid recalled that:

> There are all these arguments about money. And, 'She didn't send this' and 'They only had this kind of appetizer,' you know? My god! Is this really what people are thinking? I mean right at the wedding reception people are talking about 'Whose idea of food was this?' And it's like, wow!

Rachel Greenberg continued his thought, "It's all measured up, they're measuring the worth of the marriage by the money that was spent on it." The materialistic emphasis was insulting to middle-class GLBT family members who did not receive comparable help when setting up their own households or entering into committed relationships. They were perhaps hoping to maintain their class privilege despite being oppressed as GLBT. In poor and working class families, GLBT family members did not expect such gifts, but observed that the wealthier sides of their family were passing it on. "There's a lot of anxiety and anger when it comes to somebody having a lavish wedding . . . a big part of it is the money [because my parents never had any]" (Jason Royball).

Participants discussed what it would take for heterosexual weddings to be inclusive of, and positively meaningful for, GLBT family members. Making weddings about commitment rather than any particular kind of relationship was the general theme (see Website for practical suggestions). Gillis (1996) argued that weddings are becoming more individualized and less traditional in part because brides and grooms are personalizing their ceremonies. Participants in this study, however, pointed out that "personalizing" doesn't necessarily change the meaning, or the social power behind that meaning (see also Currie, 1993). In order for weddings to truly change, participants believed that heterosexism must be resisted rather than disguised. As Jason Royball said, it will take more effort than putting "everyone in cowboy outfits."

The inclusive weddings that GLBT family members had experienced were described as similar to same-sex commitment ceremonies; they were focused on commitment rather than heterosexuality. Karen MacDonald said:

> They weren't materialistic, they weren't requesting gifts, they wrote their own vows. Actually when you think of it [the wedding was] similar

to what gay people do when they have their own commitment ceremonies: They have their own vows, it's very small, its more focused on friends . . . family was not [necessarily] invited. [There was] a lot of preparation to the ceremony and the meaning behind it rather than the parties, the gifts, the reception.

Motivations for Attendance and Nonattendance

We need to understand why people participate in the ways that they do (Comstock, 1982). Despite the inequities that they face, GLBT family members love and feel loyal towards their siblings, parents, and other relatives, and want to be supportive of their relationships: Joan Prutsman is "happy for anyone who can find a mate, be they straight, gay, or whatever." Many participants said, "Of course I would be there"; failing to attend was not an option. In some families, not showing up would have led to more conflict than showing up and suffering through the events. Over and over, participants voiced that they did not want to make a scene and take away from the bride and groom's big day. Many hoped that their loyalty and affection would be reciprocated, but few believed that this would ever happen: Jess Avery wondered:

> Would they come through and fill the role that I want them in? I don't think so [the group agrees]. I think I'd have a lonely little thing on a deserted beach somewhere, a small fire going. And that's the double exclusion; 'Yes, you must submit to what we want you to be in this ceremony, and no, we will not commit to what you want.'

The decision not to attend family weddings, or to attend only under certain conditions, was sometimes made after being mistreated. Kyle Monroe:

> decided I'm not going to any more straight weddings. I've been to a lot of them, and I can't really see any of them as a positive experience for me. . . . I've had too much of a negative experience to ever go through it again.

Most of the time, however, participants found a way to negotiate involvement. Some decided to attend only weddings where their partner was also equally included. Others, such as Debbie Miller, found polite excuses for limiting their attendance:

> I'm at the age where my nieces and nephews are getting married, and thank God I belong to a track club that runs on Saturdays! [the group

laughs]. I avoid the church, shower at the club, rush into the reception with the gift and rush out before the dance. I say, 'Glad for you! Happy day! Blah, blah, blah.'

SOCIAL AND HISTORICAL CONTEXT

An interpretive account of action, meaning, and motives is not sufficient for feminist critical science. The account must be also positioned within social and historical context (Comstock, 1982). The idea that weddings could be problematic for GLBT family members is perhaps recent. For example, Beth Stein described how different it felt to be at a family wedding in the 1970s. Attending a wedding where her partner wasn't invited "upset" her, but the meaning behind her emotions "didn't sink in for years." The lesbians that Beth associated with at that time didn't have commitment ceremonies or wear rings to show that they were in a relationship. Feeling excluded at heterosexual weddings "was just a given" back then, while today she has the expectation that she and her family should be included in their family of origin rituals. Beth's experience is congruent with Weston's (1991) analysis of the shift from GLBT people defining family as heterosexual only, to differentiating between families of origin and families of choice.

To simplify Weston (1991), as the costs of coming out (such as being arrested, institutionalized, or blacklisted) have diminished and the modern GLBT civil rights movement has grown, more GLBT people feel free to disclose their identities, and to expect that their identities and relationships will be accepted if not affirmed. The GLBT tradition of making family out of friendship and community has continued to evolve. In addition, GLBT people have increased access to alternate insemination and other routes to parenthood, and have made inroads in the area of domestic partnership benefits. Thus, not only have GLBT people come to define their own unique relationship structures as relevant to heterosexual society, but they have also inserted themselves into dominant family categories of parent, child, and spouse as openly GLBT people. This transformation has co-occurred with major changes in heterosexual family structure and the growing expectation of heterosexual people that their own diverse family forms be accepted. Even when acceptance and affirmation do not occur or are contested, and even though GLBT relationships have no legal recognition and few social privileges, the expectation is growing that they *should*. This moral imperative has opened the closet door and allowed a questioning of the relationships between heterosexism and family life. The analysis presented in this paper is made possible by this social transformation.

IMPLICATIONS

Doing heterosexism at weddings was much more complex than hiding the existence of GLBT family members. Yes, sometimes GLBT people were excluded outright, such as when they were not invited, not photographed, or not spoken to. But other times, there was more an insidious redefinition where the GLBT person was asked to change themselves so that they wouldn't have to be excluded: Wear this, say this, do that, and *then* you will be included. Often, these conditions for inclusion pressured the GLBT family member to approximate gender conformity. Thus, this research does support the idea that weddings reproduce gender relations (e.g., Cheal, 1988; Currie, 1993). It goes further, however, to complicate gender by showing its interrelationship with heterosexism (see also Pharr, 1988).

Resistance to heterosexism was also complex. Sometimes it was a simple and blatant refusal to do something. However, resistance at weddings was more likely to be indirect and socially acceptable–it was accomplished in ways that subverted but did not overtly challenge heterosexism. The prevalence of subversion, rather than more overt resistance, suggests that GLBT people have partially accommodated themselves to heterosexism within their families of origin. This suggests that GLBT family members do sometimes compromise their own well-being in order to preserve family ties. Given the tenacity and pervasiveness of heterosexism in our society, and the expectation of front-stage behavior (Goffman, 1959) at weddings, it is not surprising that GLBT family members found it difficult, or even incomprehensible, to consider directly challenging mistreatment meted out by their families. This does not mean that GLBT people deserve or enjoy being marginalized. Rather, it speaks to the power of heterosexism to create a situation in which GLBT people have double binds rather than choices: If you are real, you may lose your family. If you hide, you may lose yourself.

The double binds experienced by GLBT people suggest that they inhabit a paradoxical position within their families of origin, and within the wedding itself (in contrast to unmarried heterosexual people who may feel excluded by a wedding, but not by their family of origin). Patricia Hill-Collins (1991) described *outsider within* as the position of being subjugated in a social situation where dominant cultural norms are being acted out and insiders fail to notice, much less question, your subjugation. The *outsider within* understands the inside rules, but also understands the power-relations behind those rules and what alternative realities they obscure. As *outsiders within*, GLBT family members bring our attention to within-family diversity.

We need to move beyond the assumption that families are either straight or gay. Most current research on GLBT relationships focuses on the romantic and parenting relationships that gay and lesbian adults create (e.g., Kurdek, 1993; Patterson, 1992). This research is extremely important. At the same time, it should be noted that people have families of origin and families of creation that incorporate both heterosexual and GLBT members (cf. Crosbie-Burnett, Foster, Murray, & Bowen, 1996; Weston, 1991). Empirical work in this area has tremendous potential for the development of more inclusive family theory. An example is my study of young women's social networks after a young woman came out to herself as bisexual or lesbian (Oswald, 2000). Coming out transformed not only the newly bisexual or lesbian woman, but also her heterosexual siblings, parents, friends, lovers, and coworkers, and their relationships with each other. By exploring GLBT and heterosexual loved ones in relation to each other, we avoid setting up gay versus straight dichotomies, and instead are able to see how each affects the other. Future research should be designed to account for multiple perceptions of the same phenomena.

Although this study sampled only GLBT people, it is important to investigate whether, and how, heterosexism shape the lives of heterosexual people. Participants in this study offered a vision of weddings that was based on commitment rather than heterosexuality or material benefits. The critique underlying this vision reveals distaste for hetero-normative scripts that may be shared by heterosexual people. What is the experience of heterosexual people at weddings? Do they also feel hollow? Overly materialistic? What values are driving their vision of relationships? We need comparative research that locates the experiences of heterosexual people within a heterosexist context.

Finally, a note about policy. Although a link between the socio-political and the interpersonal was made, perceptions of interpersonal dynamics were emphasized. This emphasis reflects my intention to offer information that practitioners can readily apply to their work with families. It would be a mistake, however, to not consider the implications for policy. Participants continually explained the quality of interaction between themselves and members of their families of origin as shaped by the legal and socially accepted derogation of GLBT relationships and identities. This suggests that when we debate marriage rights, or any other policy issue that shapes the lives of GLBT people, their partners and children, we need to remember that the parents, grandparents, siblings, cousins, aunts, and uncles of GLBT people are also being affected. Any family policy should be assessed for its impact on both heterosexual and GLBT people, and an equal distribution of benefits should be one criterion for success.

REFERENCES

Baumann, G. (1992). Ritual implicates "others": Reading Durkheim in a plural society. In D. DeCoppet (Ed.), *Understanding rituals* (pp. 97-116). New York: Routledge.

Braithwaite, D. (1995). Ritualized embarrassment at coed wedding and baby showers. *Communication Reports, 8*(2), 145-157.

Braithwaite, D., & Baxter, L. (1995). 'I do' again: The relational dialectics of renewing marriage vows. *Journal of Social and Personal Relationships, 12*(2), 177-198.

Cheal, D. (1988). Relationships in time: Ritual, social structure, and the life course. *Studies in Symbolic Interaction, 9*, 83-109.

Comstock, D. (1982). A method for critical research. In E. Bredo & W. Feinberg (Eds.), *Knowledge and values in social and educational research* (pp. 370-390). Philadelphia: Temple University Press.

Crosbie-Burnett, M., Foster, T., Murray, C., & Bowen, G. (1996). Gays' and lesbians' families-of-origin: A social-cognitive-behavioral model of adjustment. *Family Relations, 45*(4), 397-403.

Currie, D. (1993). Here comes the bride: The making of a "modern traditional" wedding in western culture. *Journal of Comparative Family Studies, 24*(3), 403-421.

Demo, D., & Allen, K. (1996). Diversity within lesbian and gay families. *Journal of Social and Personal Relationships, 13*(3), 415-434.

Federal Defense of Marriage Act. (1996). H.R. 3396. http://www.lectlaw.com/files/leg23.htm.

Gillis, J. (1996). *A world of their own making: Myth, ritual, and the quest for family values*. Cambridge, MA: Harvard University Press.

Goffman, E. (1959). *The presentation of self in everyday life*. New York: Anchor Books.

Harraway, D. (1990). A manifesto for cyborgs: Science, technology, and socialist feminism in the 1980's. In L. Nicholson (Ed.), *Feminism: Postmodernism*. New York: Routledge.

Hill-Collins, P. (1991). Learning from the outsider-within: The sociological significance of Black feminist thought. In M. Fonow & J. Cook (Eds.), *Beyond methodology: Feminist scholarship as lived experience* (pp. 35-59). Bloomington, IN: Indiana University Press.

Krueger, R. (1994). *Focus groups: A practical guide for applied research*. Thousand Oaks, CA: Sage.

Kurdek, L. (1993). The allocation of household labor in gay, lesbian, and heterosexual married couples. *Journal of Social Issues, 49*(3), 127-139.

LaRossa, R., & Reitzes, D. (1993). Symbolic interactionism and family studies. In P. Boss, W. Doherty, R. LaRossa, W. Schumm, & S. Steinmetz (Eds.), *Sourcebook of family theories and methods: A contextual approach* (pp. 135-163). New York: Plenum Press.

Lather, P. (1991). *Getting smart: Feminist research and pedagogy with/in the postmodern*. New York: Routledge.

Osmond, M., & Thorne, B. (1993). Feminist theories: The social construction of gender in families and society. In P. Boss, W. Doherty, R. LaRossa, W. Schumm, & S.

Steinmetz (Eds.), *Sourcebook of family theories and methods: A contextual approach* (pp. 591-622). New York: Plenum Press.

Oswald, R. (2000). Relationships change when young women come out as bisexual or lesbian. *Journal of Homosexuality, 38*(3), 65-83.

Parkin, D. (1992). Ritual as spatial direction and bodily division. In D. DeCoppet (Ed.), *Understanding rituals* (pp. 11-25). New York: Routledge.

Patterson, C. (1992). Children of lesbian and gay parents. *Child Development, 63*, 1025-1042.

Pharr, S. (1988). *Homophobia: A weapon of sexism.* Inverness, CA: Chardon Press.

Rediger, S. (1996). Critical theory research: The emancipatory interest in family therapy. In D. Sprenkle & S. Moon (Eds.), *Research methods in family therapy* (pp. 127-144). New York: Guilford Press.

Rettig, K., Tam, V., & Yellowthunder, L. (1995). Family policy and critical science research: Facilitating change. *Journal of Family and Economic Issues, 16*(1), 109-143.

Roberts, J. (1988). Setting the frame: Definitions, functions, and typology of rituals. In E. Imber-Black, J. Roberts, & E. Whiting (Eds.), *Rituals in families and family therapy* (pp. 3-46). New York: W.W. Norton.

Rust, P. (1993). 'Coming out' in the age of social constructionism: Sexual identity formation among lesbian and bisexual women. *Gender and Society, 7*(1), 50-77.

Rust, P. (1992). The politics of sexual identity: Sexual attraction and behavior among lesbian and bisexual women. *Social Problems, 39*(4), 366-386.

Strauss, A., & Corbin, J. (1991). *Basics of qualitative research: Grounded theory procedures and techniques.* Newbury Park, CA: Sage.

West, C, & Zimmerman, D. (1987). Doing gender. *Gender and Society, 1*, 125-151.

Weston, K. (1991). *Families we choose: Lesbians, gays, kinship.* New York: Columbia University Press.

Index

African Americans, commitment
    rituals, 49-70
Anarchism, 37-40

Boal, Augusto, 40-42
Butler, Judith, 42-45

Camp Sister Spirit (Mississippi), 85-106
    discussion, 102-104
    establishment, 88-91
    patterns of sado-ritual syndrome,
       92-102. *See also* Sado-ritual
       syndrome
Childlessness, as choice, 24-25
Circle of Mothers ritual, 23-24
Coming out, 1-6
    as (be)coming, 34-37
    Dianic ritual for, 25-26
    Jewish ritual and, 31-33
Commitment rituals. *See also*
       Weddings; Wedding study
    analysis, 55-60
    communitas and, 61-67
    discussion, 67-68
    name change study, 71-83
    personal and social transformation,
       60-61
    shower and holy union ceremony,
       52-55
    study design, 51-52
Communitas, 61-67
Conspiracy theory, 86
Consumerism, at commitment
    ceremonies, 58-59
Critical science, feminist, 109-110,113

Daly, Mary, 85-106
Death and grieving, 7-14
Defense of Marriage Act, 50
Diana (Roman Goddess), 19-20
Dianic tradition, 15-28
    childlessness in, 24-25
    Circle of Mothers ritual, 23-24
    coming out, 25-26
    embodiment concept, 22
    heterosexuals in, 19
    history, 15-18
    reflection on, 28
    rites of passage (Women's
       Mysteries), 18

Engagement announcements, 4

Factitive order, 59-60
Family of origin, weddings and
    heterosexism, 107-131
Family reconciliation, 7-14
Feminist critical science, 109-110
Feminist spirituality, 15-28

Goldman, Emma, 38
Grieving, 7-14
Gyn/Ecology (Daly), 86-87

Healing rituals, 7-14
Heterosexism
    as compared with heterosexuality,
       115